Hook, Line, and Sinker

To order additional copies of
Hook, Line, and Sinker, by Heather Marie Thompson,
call **1–800–765–6955**.

Visit us at
www.AutumnHousePublishing.com
for information on other Autumn House® products.

How to Keep From Swallowing Popular Myths

Hook, Line, and Sinker

A PRACTICAL GUIDE to DATING and RELATING

Heather Marie Thompson

Autumn House® Publishing
www.autumnhousepublishing.com
A Division of REVIEW AND HERALD® PUBLISHING
Since 1861

Published by Autumn House® Publishing, a division of Review and Herald® Publishing, Hagerstown, MD 21741-1119

Autumn House® titles may be purchased in bulk for educational, business, fund-raising, or sales promotional use. For information, please e-mail SpecialMarkets@reviewandherald.com.

Autumn House® Publishing publishes biblically based materials for spiritual, physical, and mental growth and Christian discipleship.

The author assumes full responsibility for the accuracy of all facts and quotations as cited in this book.

This book was
Edited by Kalie Kelch
Copyedited by Tarah Benton
Designed by Trent Truman
Cover art © istockphoto.com
Interior designed by Heather Rogers
Typeset: Bembo 11.5/13.5

PRINTED IN U.S.A.

5   4   3   2   1

Library of Congress Cataloging-in-Publication Data
Thompson, Heather, 1987-   .
   Hook, line, and sinker : a practical guide to dating and relating / Heather Thompson.
      p. cm.
   At head of title: How to keep from swallowing popular myths
   Includes bibliographical references and index.
1. Single women—Religious life. 2. Dating (Social custom)—Religious aspects—Christianity. 3. Mate selection—Religious aspects—Christianity. I. Title. II. Title: How to keep from swallowing popular myths.
   BV4596.S5T45 2011
   241'.6765082—dc22
                                    2010033814

ISBN 978-0-8127-0504-1

Contents

Chapter 1   There's a Big Difference Between
a Lightning Bug and a Lightning Bolt 7

Chapter 2   It's Not About Finding a Boyfriend—
It's About Building a Team 14

Chapter 3   If He Says He's "Not That Guy,"
He Is Definitely That Guy..22

Chapter 4   Don't Be the Jealous Girlfriend 29

Chapter 5   If You Guys Aren't Laughing,
You're Wasting Each Other's Time............................37

Chapter 6   If It Didn't Work the Last Three Times,
This Time Won't Be Different 44

Chapter 7   If Your Net Catches a Lightning Bug,
Set Him Free...52

Chapter 8   R-E-S-P-E-C-T: Respect 59

Chapter 9   If You Think He's The One, Take It Slow 65

Chapter 10   Cheating . . . Pretty Much a Deal Breaker.................69

Chapter 11   Let's Talk About Sex 76

Chapter 12   The Calm Before the Storm 85

Chapter 13   You Know That You've Been Struck When 89

There's a Big Difference Between a Lightning Bug and a Lightning Bolt

No boyfriend, good boyfriend, bad boyfriend, dumped—you name it, and I've lived it. It's only now in my life that I've discovered the antidote for relational success. I wish I could have learned this earlier, but whatever you do, don't settle!

Let's be serious. We've all had that heinously nerve-wrenching moment where we look at our lives and wonder, what if I never meet someone? What if I never get that miraculous sign from God where the Lord Himself points out my future mate and yells in my ear, "Get ready! This is the one!" What if He doesn't do that for me? What if I miss the signs?

Because we're filled with these fears and insecurities, we settle. We decide that good is good enough and we'll take what we can get. Well, I'm a firm believer that there's a big difference between a lightning bug and a lightning bolt. I'm not sure who first said that—maybe it was Shakespeare or Forrest Gump—but either way, it's the truth.

There are thousands of lightning bugs in the dating world—people who make you turn your head and smile. Our friends often recommend these lightning bugs to us because they are our "type." Heck, you can go outside in July and catch a jarful of them if you want to. Realistically, however, we are better off leaving them in our backyards. The problem comes when we confuse these "bugs" for bolts. Lightning usually only strikes once in a lifetime, and when it hits, the "bugs" scatter like leaves in the wind.

I don't have a degree in psychology nor would I dub myself the queen of relational wisdom. I am sharing with you nothing more than common sense based on a life full of great, and not-so-great experiences. I also know what it's like being a Christian and trying to figure out where you stand and what you want out of a perspective partner. It isn't easy, but life usually never is.

Trying to find a balance between what secular society portrays as a picture-perfect relationship and what you know as a Christian is hard. My only prayer is that this book will give you a small dose of common sense along with a large helping of good old-fashioned late-night slumber party wisdom. Think of this book as a sort of informative dating diary. Walk a mile in my high heels and avoid all the left turns that made me stumble. Hopefully, when all is said and done, not only will you be well on your way to snagging your soul mate but lightning will be close behind.

Here's the truth—I'm going to be blunt because anything else would be confusing—if you have to ask yourself what lightning means, you probably haven't been struck. A lightning bolt in my analogy is true love. It's Romeo and Juliet—but with a less fatal ending. Love (and I believe true love can only be acquired once you love Christ first) is unmistakable. It's not gone in a blink of an eye or blown in the wind. It's permanent, like words once they're said or first impressions. Once it's acknowledged, there's no going back. That's the good news. Once we are in it, we're playing for keeps, and therein lies the bad news.

Often, especially in today's day and age, love and marriage, the ultimate symbolism of love, are viewed more like a telephone number. It's great if it lasts, but if things get sticky and you need a fast break, you can always start over and get a new one. If you have some bad experiences and would rather cut your losses, you have the freedom to do so, regardless of whether the change leaves one of you permanently out of service. God, however, insists that marriage is sacred. It's not something you throw the towel in on because things get a little sweaty.

In fact, the first time we read about God's view on marriage it seems almost irreversible. Genesis 2:23 and 24 says, "The man said, 'This is now bone of my bones, And flesh of my flesh; She shall be called Woman, because she was taken out of Man,' For this reason a man shall leave his father and his mother, and be joined to his wife; and they shall become one flesh."

This is not something to take lightly. God says you will become one flesh, one body, and one person. Your two souls will intertwine, and your hearts will beat rhythmically. To cut flesh apart from flesh seems almost inconceivable, and if it happens, the experience leaves tremendous scars.

I'm not here to debate the biblical grounds of divorce. I only want to stress the importance of the very thing you may be rushing to find. It's not a new telephone number you're signing a contract for, it's the admittance of another person's soul within yours. You can't rush that. It isn't worth it. That's something that can only be found in God's time.

Now that you have a better idea on how important the subject we are speaking of actually is, we can start at the beginning. This realization actually took me a long time to learn, but since I've grasped it, I've been changed. I believe you cannot fall in love with a man without first falling in love with the Creator of man.

Jesus Christ is the best picture we have of what love truly is. You can't know what love is like without first knowing Him. God is love. He is the epitome of self-sacrifice, the provider for miraculous enlightenment, the initiator of merciful forgiveness, the representation of phenomenal groundbreaking loyalty, and the Creator of undeniably life-changing truth. Our society tells us that actions speak louder than words—the action of Christ's sacrifice on the cross is deafening.

If you don't understand that first, if you don't see what God says you deserve, you wouldn't recognize lightning if it struck you in broad daylight. You wouldn't recognize it because you would have nothing to measure it by. You'd find yourself mistaking every lightning bug, whether dim or bright, for the real deal. If you don't first appreciate the author of love, you'll never find value in the tangible gift He placed on this earth just for your sake—the other half of your heart.

So please, rest assured that God won't let you miss such a life-altering event as meeting your future spouse. But in order for God to lead you, you must be in tune with His guidance. Prayer is an important step in ensuring your meeting with destiny. As an example, you wouldn't sit by the window every day waiting for a package you never ordered. In the same light, you need to talk with God if you think you're ready for Him to deliver. God promises that if we ask for something according to His will, it is given to us.

The Bible says, "This is the confidence we have in approaching God: that if we ask anything according to his will, he hears us. And if we know that he hears us—whatever we ask—we know that we have what we asked of him" (1 John 5:14, 15).

Certainly then, your prayer to meet the person God has planned for you will be granted. I'm sure that prayer is so closely tied into His will that it's double knotted. Once you ask God to take control, there is no going back. You can't ask God to get involved and then send Him away because you don't like His response. You can't do that. Not without severing the ties you created with Him through prayer. God has seen firsthand the importance that the role of the person you make part of your life takes. He watched Adam fall for the sake of Eve, and if He can help it, together you can ensure that history, at least in your life, does not repeat itself.

While in school, I had a professor who changed my thinking, and just by speaking, he held me accountable to never settle. He used to talk about how much he loved his wife. I loved hearing him talk about her because it always rekindled my faith that true love wasn't just an ending for fairy tales. When he spoke of marriage, he always said that if you got that one aspect of your life right everything else could be wrong and none of it would matter. And in contrast, if you got that one aspect of your life wrong, everything else could be right yet none of it would matter. I used to ponder that philosophy and contemplate its validity.

I then wondered what happened when people simply settled. Many people, especially women, sense their biological clock ticking and jump into a marriage drastically different than the one they envisioned from childhood. They take the frog over the prince because at least then they have security. They stick it out in dead-end relationships because the thought of starting over with someone new seems worse than the thought of never being truly happy. I thought about all these things, and then I got to know God, and then I didn't wonder anymore.

I'm going to say it again—don't settle. It is not part of God's plan for you to settle. The person who you are supposed to spend the rest of your life with will in a large way become the person you turn out to be. Your goals will be either made or broken by their goals, and your dreams will be pushed or crushed in their hands. Wisely pick the hand you want to hold your future because you only get one shot.

Take some notes from me—there have been many times in my life that I almost settled for lightning bugs. I have encountered three very serious and very long-term bugs who I actually thought would be the fathers of my children. I did this not once, not twice, but three times! Looking back, I realize that I only thought that because I wanted to be done. I was tired of the dating game. I wanted security, and when I found it, I clung to it. Had God not first found me, I would have been married three times by now to three great men who just wouldn't have been great for me.

Luckily I realized, and actually quite suddenly, that after all the years I had invested in these relationships God was pulling me elsewhere. It's funny because I can honestly tell you that every time I prayed, and I mean sincerely prayed, for God's will to be done, He did it. I could be in the middle of a long-term relationship that was running smoothly toward a wedding aisle and the second I asked God for His opinion everything was turned upside down. All of a sudden my smooth road became bumpy, and I began rolling downhill. The crash is always inevitable, and although it hurts, I'd pick it any day compared to a lifetime without fulfillment.

I have to admit that it has been because of those flames that I have been afraid to ask God for His help in other relationships. Sometimes I'd meet someone I was awed by. Someone who was filled with all the right qualities that I was certain would make us a dynamic team. I'd meet this person, and I'd be afraid for God to tell me the truth. I was afraid that He would take away my wings before I had a chance to make them flutter. I was afraid that what I wanted wouldn't match up with what He wanted and that I'd be alone again.

I can remember one specific instance when I had just gotten done bragging to my friends about my new boyfriend at the moment when I decided it was time to ask God for a little input. I can recite for you my prayer almost word for word because I was sincere as I spoke it and just as sincerely nervous for His answer. My prayer went like this: "God, I really like this guy. I think we could change the world together. I see a future, but if you don't, then just set fire to it before it goes any farther and I truly invest my heart."

Almost before I could say amen a friend of mine called me with terrible news. The guy, the same guy I had conjured up to be almost mythical, had not only hit on her but he had said some pretty awful things about me. The whole thing ended in me losing my cool (which by the way, if you're going to lose that, you may as well throw your dignity away) and resulted in a night filled with tears.

As I cried, I realized that the entire ordeal was bittersweet. Sure, it stung at the time, but the upside was that God had heard me. Not only had He heard me but He also really cared about my life. So much so that He protected me from something that may seem as trivial to us as a boyfriend. God interceded on my behalf, and from then on, I was changed.

If you ask God to be a part of every aspect of your life, He will be. In fact, He wants to be. Never feel like anything is too big or too small to bring before His throne. There is no one else in this entire universe who has your best interest at heart quite like He does.

A friend of mine once read me a quote that says that there is an incredible difference between saying prayers and praying. You can quickly mumble a rehearsed prayer that sounds good but just scrapes the surface of your heart. If you want to seriously begin breaking new ground, you have to dig deeper than the surface and strike oil in your heart. You have to be willing to accept both the good and the bad or else this will never work for you. You could probably avoid a lot of bad things if you stop choosing things for yourself and begin allowing Him to choose for you.

Keep that in mind as you read this book and as you talk to God about this topic. God heard my prayer that day because He knew I was genuine. He knew that despite what I wanted I was prepared to let Him break me because what He had was going to fit me much better. Often our vision for our lives is so limited in comparison to what God actually has in store if we allow Him full control. You are truly only cheating yourself not to allow Him that control.

As we finish this chapter, let's look at the three P's of dating.

1. Prayer. First, tell God what you want and what you're looking for. Then, sit back and listen to what He has to tell you. Without asking God to get involved, you are fighting a losing battle. Any preconceived notions, any prior selections, and any previous thoughts have to be thrown out the window if it was done by your own brainpower. This can't work, and won't work, if He's not your matchmaker.

2. Patience. This is probably the biggest step to the most important decision you will ever make in your life. Since so much of what you will actually do with your life is tied into whom you spend your life with, you can't afford to rush things. You don't have the luxury to deal with those repercussions. Take your time!

3. Please, do not settle! No matter who you are, where you're from, or what you look like, there is no reason for you to ever settle for less than extraordinary. Besides, when you settle you are settling not only for a love without passion but a life without

faith. Settling says to God that you don't have enough confidence that He'll pull through in the clutch. It says that you think He may forget about you or may become too busy to bring you your soul mate.

I can assure you that love is God's specialty, and weddings are His favorite kind of party. He is never "too busy" to align the stars for you, so don't settle for a small yard when He's already purchased the deed on several acres. If anything, sit back, be patient, and listen for the thunder.

It's Not About Finding a Boyfriend—It's About Building a Team

If you go into a relationship with a relationship mentality, that's all it will ever be. You are not looking for a relationship. That's what your backyard and a jar with air holes is for, remember? You are looking for your husband. And once the word marriage enters the picture, your standards immediately have to change. Your standards have to change because you aren't just looking for a swing-set romance. You want more than comfortable and better then average; you should be aiming higher then happy.

Happy won't be enough to get you through tear-stained arguments and business trips apart. Trust me, I have been "happy" more times then I have fingers. If happy is all you are looking for, you might as well bait your hook and cast your line anywhere. Happy is everywhere. It's like relational fleas; anyone can catch it. Most marriages start out happy. Most people could settle and be happy with almost anyone. Happy is normal.

Dictionary.com defines happy as "characterized by or indicative of pleasure, contentment, or joy." It's standard. It's a really nice-looking lightning bug. It's nice to have, but it may not leave you feeling fulfilled. Being happily married may not be all it's cracked up to be. Happy is an ending for fairy tales; you want to hook extraordinary. Dictionary.com defines extraordinary as "beyond what is usual." It's more than what you ever expected. Being struck by lightning is "beyond what is usual."

One of my favorite movies of all time is the 2005 hit comedy romance *Hitch*. The movie is about a so-called love doctor named Alex 'Hitch' Hitchins. Played by Will Smith, Hitch holds the view that any man, at any time, can sweep any woman off her feet. The premise is that Hitch goes around helping other men get a shot at true love, but he ends up falling in love himself. After some altercations between him and his point of admiration, Sara, the two end up calling it quits.

My favorite line in the movie is where Hitch corners Sara in the stairwell of her apartment building and begs for her to stay with him. She looks him in the eyes and says, "Like you said, if we go our separate ways, we'll do just fine."

And Hitch, who before had sworn off love for himself, looks at her and genuinely replies, "But what if I don't want fine? What if I want extraordinary?" Do yourself a favor, and settle for nothing short of extraordinary.

Relationships are temporary. They can be here today and gone tomorrow. They can be fleeting and pointless and merely for the purpose of occupying some extra time. If that's where your head is at, I suggest you pick up a different book. The problem with today's society is that marriage is viewed as simply another relationship. It's expendable and can be jumped into and leaped out of with not much more thought than the blink of an eye. Even the word relationship lacks commitment.

You are not looking for a boyfriend—you are getting ready to meet your spouse. As a Christian, you need to uphold the value system you know to be true. You are wasting your time if you're simply seeking out relationships. You need to be focused on the prize. You are in the business of building a successful team. Once you realize this, and truly digest it, dating becomes 50 percent easier. It's easier because you can say goodbye to the "maybes" and the "fixer uppers." All you have to do now is allow yourself to be swept off your feet by perfection.

Remember, all you want in the dating saga is to be struck by lightning. That's it. That's the dream. In that one defining moment, all the puzzle pieces will seem to make sense. You will understand why it never worked with anyone else and why now was the only time you could have, or should have, been hit. Just like I wouldn't give scissors to a 5-year-old to cut her own hair, God doesn't send thunder until we're ready for it.

That's probably the hardest part. The blind trust we have to place in Him to provide for us. We can't always see the whole picture. In fact, we rarely can. It's hard for us, especially for those of us who are controlling people by nature, to sit back and be patient.

I, by nature, am not a patient person. That virtue is probably the hardest thing for me to learn. Because I am not patient, I would constantly jump into relationships with people who I knew were temporary. Perhaps this was the cause of my long-term battle with destiny. Maybe God simply wanted me to sit still long enough to put my faith in Him rather then trying to solve all my problems myself.

In the end the relationships that I jumped into as a quick fix or time filler only thwarted me on my path to finding the person I was actually supposed to be with. Little did I know that I was wasting my time, and it was distracting me from what I needed to be paying attention to. It kept me from spending time by myself to figure out exactly what made me tick and thus get a clearer picture as to what I was looking for. It kept me from trusting.

Every time you get into a relationship, whether wholeheartedly or halfheartedly, it takes a toll on you. What if you aren't ready when your soul mate walks through the door because you're busy breaking up with someone you should have never been with in the first place? Time is valuable. I don't think I realized that until much later in my life, and even then I made mistakes. I wish I had understood that from the beginning; I could have saved myself a lot of unnecessary heartache. I could have hurt less people by not dragging them into the mess that was me. I could have been a better Christian, and I could've put someone else's feelings before my own had I just been patient.

So let's talk about building a successful team and how you know what you should be looking for in another team member. Again, I can only speak out of my personal experiences, and I can only give you honesty. In my life as a Christian dater, one of the biggest challenges I've faced is the compatibility of religions. Your belief systems should be what keeps you grounded in a storm and what gives you comfort in times of tragedy. Your personal religious beliefs should be one of the biggest factors in who you are, thus making an even bigger factor in deciding who you should be with.

Your belief in God and individual vision of who He is and what He has revealed to you should be your most guarded treasure. The only truth you can go by is what you feel the Holy Spirit has placed on your heart. Therefore, your beliefs, whatever they may be, should be worn upon your heart.

One of the most important things to remember is that dating should not be your chance for evangelism. Trust me on this one; I was a habitual offender. You should never go into a relationship hoping to change the other person's religion or work around your religious differences. This is your life, and your children's future. It is not a game to be won nor should it be a method of conversion. If your relationship faces serious denominational differences, you should leave it in the realm of friendship.

I am not just saying this because of what my parents taught me. I am saying it because I was madly in love with a man who was a different religion than me. I loved him so much that I tried to convict him of my truth. I was engaged to him and wanted nothing more than to be his wife. Two months before our wedding, I was feeling uneasy and was praying to God at every spare moment for a sign that I was making the right decision. I begged Him to speak to me, and then I realized that He had been all along; I just didn't want to hear it. I do that a lot to God—tune Him out. It's a good thing that God is so invested in who we are in spite of what we may do. He interceded for me, and all of a sudden our religious differences, that I had convinced myself were minor, blew up like a chemistry experiment.

My heart was broken. I was humiliated. The truth is it blew up so quickly that I didn't even know what hit me. If you think breaking up is painful, try breaking up and then having to tell all your wedding guests about it. I felt like the whole world was whispering behind my back, even though I am sure it was all in my head. I could barely walk past my closet for fear that that dumb wedding dress would poke its head out and laugh at me. I realize now that I was lucky.

It's never too late to do an about-face and give God back the reins. There is nothing you can do to disappoint God so badly that He doesn't want to deal with you and your drama anymore. Take it from me, a person who has been the worst backseat driver He has probably ever seen—He will always take you back. No matter how bad the collision, how bleak the wreck, He'll make you new.

Religious differences are best worked out in the realm of friendship. Through prayer, study, and meditation, you will know what truth is. God calls us to be faithful to Him and the biblical truths that He has given us. Don't compromise your beliefs. Marriage has enough challenges; don't join yourself with someone who will not add to your beliefs but will perhaps tear you away from them.

God made this point clear through Abraham as he spoke about Isaac, implying that marrying outside of his faith was not permitted: "I want you to swear by the Lord, the God of heaven and the God of earth, that you will not get a wife for my son from the daughters of the Canaanites, among whom I am living, but will go to my country and my own relatives and get a wife for my son Isaac" (Gen. 24:3, 4).

Hundreds of years later, when Moses spoke to the children of Israel before they entered the Promised Land, he reinforced the same idea: "Do not intermarry with them. Do not give your daughters to their sons or take their daughters for your sons, for they will turn your sons away from following me to serve other gods, and the Lord's anger will burn against you and will quickly destroy you" (Deut. 7:3, 4).

I think the point of this prescription is to not put yourself in a position to be changed if you truly believe God is where your religion is. If whatever denominational practices you are involved in is where you sense Christ, don't flirt with fire. This is not to say that one person is wrong and another person is right, it's simply to say that consistency in worship is important. Though the verse on being unequally yoked explicitly refers to Christians and non-Christians, the metaphor is heavy and should be applied regardless: "Do not be yoked together with unbelievers. For what do righteousness and wickedness have in common? Or what fellowship can light have with darkness?" (2 Cor. 6:14).

The symbol that I think is important to notice here is the description of marriage as two yokes. A yoke is a large wooden crosspiece that binds the necks of two oxen together. A chain also connects the oxen so that every move they make, they make together. To have a marriage that is unequally yoked means to have a chain that doesn't fit or to have one ox walking left while the other is walking right. That will never work. Neither ox will ever move anywhere. Instead, they will tug one another into opposite directions without ever getting any work accomplished.

That image should grab your attention. It kind of takes us back to our "flesh of flesh" and "bone of bone" saying. It shows us how important marriage is, and it reminds us that as a team we'll have to move in sync with one another. The entire purpose of this life is to get yourself to heaven and take as many people with you as possible. That's it. That is the powerful and ever-so-diligently sought after meaning of life. Since God is supposed to be the key part to discovering whom it is we are supposed to marry, your religious values must also coincide.

The next step to locating the perfect partner to build your team with is taking a look at his future goals. What are they? It doesn't really matter whether or not they are similar to yours. The two of you may be vastly different or vastly the same. What is important, however, is whether or not they are demanding the same things out of life as you are. If you are seeking to change the world, it may be hard for you to be satisfied with someone who is just trying to make it till tomorrow.

If you are a go-getter and the only place he wants to go is the quickest route to easy street, he is probably not the person God knew you would need to stay motivated. And it goes both ways. We are all wired differently. That doesn't make any of us more important than the other it's just that God has different tasks for each of us. While some people are meant to be the invokers of large masses and the leaders of huge movements, others of us are meant to be the lifelong testaments of routine Christian practice. In other words, some of us are the hammers, and others the nails. Who's to say which is more important? It takes both working together to hang the picture on the wall of Christ's kingdom.

It's important to remember that the closest to God someone else may get is you, and the best way to show Christ's love is to simply be a friend. However, these differences do matter. It's important to find someone who is strong where you may be weak. It may be easier to figure out what you are looking for in someone else after you figure out exactly what it is you have to offer. Make a list of your strengths and weaknesses and how each of them may affect what God's mission is for you. Once you have your list, compare it with the person you think may be your other half. Do the lists provide a balance? Your lives should compliment each other; all the while, keep in mind the main purpose for life—heaven.

God instills in us the importance of companionship in the very second chapter of the Bible. Genesis 2:18 says, "The Lord God said, 'it is not good for the man to be alone. I will make a helper suitable for him.'" God sees Adam and recognizes that he is lonely. God sees this and wants Adam to recognize it also, so He has him name the animals.

Verses 19 and 20 say, "Now the Lord God had formed out of the ground all the beasts of the field and all the birds of the air. He brought them to the man to see what he would name them; and whatever the man called each living creature, that was its name. So the man gave names to all the livestock, the birds of the air and all the beasts of the field. But for Adam no suitable helper was found."

God didn't just tell Adam he needed a woman; He wanted to show him first. He wanted him to recognize he was missing something, and once he did, He filled the void. Verses 21 and 22 continue, "So the Lord God caused the man to fall into a deep sleep; and while he was sleeping, he took one of the man's ribs and closed up the place with flesh. Then the Lord God made a woman from the rib he had taken out of the man, and he brought her to the man."

And then right there, we see the primary case of love at first sight. Adam looks upon Eve and utters the first poetic phrases in the Bible. Verse 23 concludes, "The man said, 'this is now bone of my bones and flesh of my flesh; she shall be called woman, for she was taken out of man.'"

I wanted to show you these verses to remind you that you are not crazy for obsessing over this. If you spend a large amount of your time preoccupied with this notion of a soul mate, you are not a lunatic. God meant for us to seek that state of completeness. He recognized our need for it at the beginning of time. This is important, so that you are completely vindicated in all your romantic fantasies. Just remember to be patient. It's because this is so important that you must wait until it's right.

Another important thing to remember is that you may fall head over heels. You may meet the man of your dreams, the complete caption for all your fantasies, the walking vision of your daydreams. He may be everything you've ever wanted, but that doesn't mean he's everything you actually need. For a relationship to work, he needs to love you just as much as you love him. No more, and no less. If the balance isn't equal, someone isn't getting what they deserve. This may be one of the hardest pills to swallow, learning to let the dream go.

I've personally struggled with this. At one point in my life, I thought I had met the man who fit the description of what I had been wishing for. He was handsome and charming, and he complemented every aspect of who I was like a puzzle piece perfectly placed. He was a bolt of light, and in the distance I heard thunder. For whatever reason, however, it stopped working out. A few of our differences didn't fit together quite as perfectly as I thought once I examined our pieces closer. He was perfect, and I felt closer to perfection when he was near me, and yet I had to let him go.

At some point I realized, if he is this amazing and things aren't working out, whomever God has for me is going to floor me. I stopped looking at it from the perspective that if he left I'd have to search for a replacement, and by replacement I was imagining a knock-off brand that would never be as good. I stopped viewing it that way, and I realized that if I could connect with him and he still wasn't the one for me then the person who was going to knock me off my feet. And thinking about my true soul mate made me happy. It actually made me feel excited. I had proof that true happiness was possible. My "perfect" boyfriend gave me faith and showed me exactly what I should be looking for, only better.

So how do we know when to let go of the dream? Sadly, sometimes we just can't see it. Sometimes we may be so blinded by what we want that we don't realize it's not what we need. You will never know positively whether you are with your soul mate unless you involve God in the process. Once you talk it over with Him and tell Him you are ready for His will to precede your own, the rest is easy. He'll take care of it. He's got everything under control. Don't worry about missing it, and don't try to tell God how to do His job. I can't stress to you enough how important letting go, and letting God, is in this situation. That's the key. That's everything.

If He Says He's "Not That Guy," He Is Definitely That Guy!

'm not going to hurt you"; "I swear I'm not a player"; "I promise you're different." Ladies, these taglines are warnings, not safety zones, and my glass isn't half empty—this is the reality. The only guys who actually say these things are the ones who know they need to reinforce some innocence on their exterior on an otherwise blatantly guilty interior. Any guy who tells you he is "not that guy" is describing for you exactly what type of guy he has, indeed, been.

Guys actually aren't that hard to figure out, simply because of the fact that they are pretty consistent. When a friend is dating someone we know is pulling the wool over her eyes, we see it pretty clearly. Right from the onset we have pegged him as a bad seed. It's only when the weeds are in our garden that the lines get blurry. Let me share an example with you.

When I was about 8 years old, I met my arch nemesis. I was at a church in New York because my father did various drama productions all over the country, and this weekend I found myself furious in the Big Apple. I can't even remember what her name was; all I know is that her skin was the perfect blend of mocha and crème and that her hair was something you'd see on a Greek goddess—she was the first girl I've ever hated. That, however, is not why I hated her. I hated her because she was obnoxious.

She spent the entire Sabbath and into the evening bragging about all her accomplishments. She had been on several different commercials and even landed a spot on the dynasty of child programming—*Sesame Street*. She was extremely outgoing and could sing like a canary. She followed me everywhere I went, and I envisioned taking her perfectly long hair and tying it into a noose around her neck.

Finally the show started, and I was able to get some peace without the yapping of Miss Know-It-All. Right when I thought I was home free at the end of my father's program she turned to me and asked if I'd be her pen pal. In my head I laughed hysterically, but aloud I did what every girl instinctively knows how to do when talking to their arch nemesis. I faked a smile and told her "of course!"

Before she gave me her address, she made me pinky promise I wouldn't share it with all my friends. I guess she supposed a child-like prodigy such as herself would of course have a following. After I crossed my heart with honesty, she gave me her address along with my very own autograph that I could keep, or frame, whichever I thought would be most beneficial.

I hated car rides, especially long car rides from New York back to Michigan, but I was ecstatic to be free of what I thought to be the most annoying little girl I had ever met in my life. As we piled into the car and got out of the city, my father turned to me and inquired about my new pen pal.

"I saw you made a new friend," he said, smiling and pinching my shoulder.

"She is *NOT* my friend," I responded angrily. I honestly would have pulled my hair out if I had had to listen to her hum the *Sesame Street* theme song one more time.

"That's funny that you say that," my dad said, tipping his head back, "she reminded me a lot of you."

In that moment I froze. My body surged as both my heart pounded furiously and my stomach wanted to hurl all of my Denny's dinner into my lap. How could he compare his sweet, innocent, beautiful daughter to that spawn of Satan?

It's funny, because when I thought about that little girl again and I mentioned the story to a friend, their only response at the end of my monologue was "Really? She was on *Sesame Street*? That's awesome!" As if on cue, I broke out into hives as if I was still 8 years old and still contemplating killing her. The more I thought about how much I really had hated her the more I realized why.

The town, or in our case the church, wasn't big enough for the both of us. My dad was right. She was me, and I hated her for it. I hated her because perhaps subconsciously she showed me everything about myself that I detested. She was arrogant and stubborn, as was I; she was annoying and obnoxious, as was I; she thought she was really something special, better then everyone else, and so did I. The only thing she did have that I didn't was perfect hair and flawless skin, and if I wanted to share anything with her, it would have been that. I hated her because of everything she represented, and it just so happened that in doing so I recognized that the first girl I had ever hated was me.

Now, I realize this story isn't about being fooled by the schemes of handsome men, but it is about fooling yourself. The reason I walked you down this path of memory lane is simply because I wanted to show you that it's hard to often see what is personal to you.

Sometimes we can't see our flaws because they are ours and they aren't flattering. It's like trying to see your teeth without looking in a mirror. No matter how hard you squint your eyes or wiggle your face, you never can get an image because they're too close to you. It's so deeply attached to the gums of who you are that you almost forget they're even there. That is until you see someone else with something stuck in theirs, then all of a sudden all you can think about is checking yours and making sure you're clear. Occasionally it takes seeing someone else's flaws to realize our own imperfections.

And so that's what my arch nemesis taught me—I have to first look at my own life, which is filled with faults, before I can lose patience with anyone else. It's easy for us to scold friends for poor judgment and then practice the same ill will in our own romantic lives. Just remember, the very thing you may be protesting against could be lodged right in between your own two front teeth.

OK, we can depart from the deeper analogies for a second and just take a cold, hard look at the facts. A guy who really isn't "that guy" would never tell how much of "that guy" he's not. Think about it, why would a guy who's never been "that guy" raise your suspicions? He wouldn't. He probably wouldn't even know how! The sad truth is that we usually pass by most of the good guys we know. We place them in the "friend zone" and cry to them about how much of a jerk the guy we are pursuing is. Well, if you ask me, it's time to break those chains of friendship and recognize the shoulder you've been leaning on for the amazing man he is.

I feel bad for all the potentially great husbands who get placed into the "friend zone" because of their genuineness. It's not fair. Only in a corrupt world can sincerity and emotion place you in a realm marked "not dateable." I don't mean to lead you astray. Chemistry is definitely as important as friendship, but the two are not exchangeable. They should be pressed together so tightly they become inseparable. A friend of mine once told me that chemistry is the life source of a relationship. Though I think her point is valid, I have to say I disagree. Chemistry is the match, but without the wood (friendship), the match will burn your fingers before you can remove your hand.

I once heard that love is actually friendship on fire. If the guy you are spending your time with is not first and foremost your friend, those coals won't give you enough warmth to get you through the day, nevertheless a lifetime. Friendship is probably the single most important aspect of your relationship with your future husband. He will be set apart from everyone else because he will be the person you want to run to when you're sad, and he will be the same person you think of calling first when you're ecstatic. If you want to spend the rest of your life extraordinarily happy, look for the personality, not the abs, that can keep you smiling.

Also, if it's easy for him to say certain things, he probably doesn't mean it. My dad always told me to believe about 50 percent of what a guy tells you. Now trust me, I know firsthand how hard that is. We all want to believe that we are the most beautiful, amazing, spectacular girl in someone else's life. It feels good, so we want to believe it, but it's important to remember that the true test of someone's affections is always time. Time will tell. You just have to be patient.

Try not to jump the gun and fall head over heels too quickly. Realistically, you don't even know him yet. It usually takes about a year to completely know the heart of one of your best girlfriends, and dating isn't any different. Plus, it's important to know that guys are much better at playing their cards close to their chests than we are. They can keep a façade up for a long time because they don't think as emotionally as we do. The real key here is just to be patient. You are going to have the rest of your life to spend with this person, so let him prove his worth.

As you spend time together, you will know if he is sincere. Sincerity is pretty easy to detect. The only reason we miss it is usually because we want to. We want to believe them so badly that we ignore the warning signs. Don't be someone else's conquest. You are a beautifully crafted, intelligent, and godly woman. If you are feeling unsure about your current boyfriend, spend time in prayer. Ask your family for advice, listen to your friends, and talk to other people who know him. Odds are those who love you will be able to see the things you are missing, and you will gain a deeper insight into who he truly is by talking with those who know him.

The saying goes, actions speak louder then words. I believe that the easiest way to know if your guy is "the guy" is to completely ignore all of his words and pay close attention to his actions. Within about two weeks you will have all the answers you've been waiting for. He will have exposed himself clearly, and if you have been watching things unfold without bias, you should be able to put your best foot forward. It's all about common sense and going back to the essentials. It's so basic, and so true.

Really, we don't need self-help books to tell us everything we've always known. Sometimes, however, we do need a good kick in the butt. We fall deep into the fantasy of what could be that we forget it should not be this confusing. If you are spending more time second-guessing yourself than being happy, cut your losses.

I once dated a very outgoing guy who made my knees weak. He didn't exactly fit my "type," but his personality left me reeling. I'd lose myself in our three- to four-hour-long phone conversations and spend my days telling my friends the jokes he had told me that left me laughing into the next week. I can still remember sitting down with my mother at our oak dining table and telling her that I was sure I had found my soul mate. I was even involved in a long-term relationship at the time, but everything had been pushed to the back burner because this guy made me feel like I had won the relationship lottery, and to top it off, he said all the right things.

He told me on a daily basis how beautiful I was, how much I made him laugh, and how he had never had as much fun with any other girl—he even rather quickly dropped the "love bomb" on my very impressionable ears. At any rate, I dropped everything to be with him, and by everything, I mean my two-and-a-half-year relationship, along with some good, but ignored, advice from friends.

About a month later, we spent Thanksgiving dinner together, and he came and met my entire family. To me, everything seemed to be going smoothly, but apparently he was already plotting his exit. While dropping me off at my grandma's house, out of the blue and without explanation, he made up some quick excuse about things moving "too fast" and then he was gone. I spent a very awkward ride home with my face pressed to my parents' backseat. I hoped I would wake up and discover that it had all been some horrible dream.

He didn't call me for the next eight days, which was pretty harsh compared to the daily calls that I was used to. That was the first time in my life that I had ever been so confused and tricked. I didn't want to hang out with my friends because I didn't want to hear them say "I told you so." I picked up the phone to call him probably a thousand times, but I kept putting it back down before punching in the last number. I was devastated, but I decided rather quickly that I wouldn't give him the satisfaction of knowing that he had warped me.

I knew he would be back, and I was waiting for him. I had plotted in my head the way I would pick up the phone and toss him a few choice words that let him know just how "great" I thought he was now; revenge would be mine, I was sure of it. Eight days later I was at the drive-through window of the bank when I felt my phone vibrate. Then within seconds I heard the ringtone I had been worried I would never hear again. I stared at the phone for what felt like hours but in reality was probably only a moment. Should I pick it up and let him have it? Or should I hear him out first?

After screaming loudly once to get out all my nerves, I picked up the phone and calmly said "hello" while holding my breath and waiting for his reply.

"It's been awhile," he said quickly with the same charm and charismatic tone that had made me lose all my wits the month before.

"Yeah, it has. What have you been doing?" I said coolly, not wanting to show him how many times I had already imagined this conversation in my mind.

"I miss you, Heather," he said, unfolding his plan of pretending nothing had ever happened.

"Well then, where have you been?" I said still calmly, yet firmly, showing him I would not be taking this whole thing lying down.

"I guess I got scared," he answered.

"Scared?" I said. "If you got scared, it was your own fault. I never pushed anything on you. I wasn't the one confessing my love or calling you multiple times a day. If you got scared, it is no one's fault but your own."

Well, that weekend he showed up at the same get-together I was at. He drove an hour to see me, and it was as if those eight days, all of a sudden, were just eight days and not the years of separation and anxiety I had created them into being. We didn't get back together, but I didn't hate him anymore for not calling me. Instead, we became friends, which is what should have happened before anything else did.

The point I want to make here is this: even if he was my soul mate, he couldn't have been right then because he wasn't my friend first. We tried to skip all the important steps that make a relationship so beautiful, and I was angry when it crumbled in my hands and slipped through my fingers. Building a loving relationship without first building friendship is like building your house on sand.

Now, as much as I'd like to take credit for this easy-to-understand analogy, it was Jesus who said it first as He explained the importance of a good foundation.

In Matthew 7:24-27 Jesus explained, "Therefore everyone who hears these words of mine and puts them into practice is like a wise man who built his house on the rock. The rain came down, the streams rose, and the winds blew and beat against that house; yet it did not fall, because it had its foundation on the rock. But everyone who hears these words of mine and does not put them into practice is like a foolish man who built his house on sand. The rain came down, the streams rose, and the winds blew and beat against that house, and it fell with a great crash."

Now, when Jesus told this parable, he was speaking to the people about the importance of recognizing true spiritual beacons by their fruit. In my allegory, I encourage you to build true love on a rock—a solid and firm foundation of friendship. True friendship is not easily dismissed. It says that you care for someone else's well-being more than your own. It says that you are there for them, and care for them, and place their concerns heavily on your heart. What better person could there possibly be for you to say your vows to than your best friend?

Don't Be the Jealous Girlfriend!

Trust me when I say this, do not—I repeat, *do not*—make a fool of yourself by letting that ugly head of jealousy poke into your potentially amazing relationship. Jealousy is pretty much a synonym for insecurity. It's never attractive and completely unnecessary. Don't forget how amazing and beautiful you are. Yeah, you are not perfect, but if he's the right guy, to him you are, and that's all that matters. If you are constantly getting jealous, it could be one of two problems. Either you are extremely insecure and it's no one else's fault but your own, or he is doing it on purpose. Some guys will purposely try to make you jealous because of the same reason that you get jealous—they are insecure and are soothed by your emotional outbursts of jealousy.

If this is happening at the beginning of your relationship, it could be fair to say that your relationship is still immature. But if you have been together for a year and are still having these issues, I think you need to figure out the source of the problem. If it is you, you need to ask him to help you with it. Tell him you realize you are insecure and have a problem, and if he could remind you that you have nothing to worry about, that would be appreciated. Let's jog down the road into the future. If you don't deal with this you'll end up at a complete dead-end.

No one wants to stay with someone who is constantly insecure. That just gets annoying. Let us also not forget that you are looking for your soul mate, not a boyfriend. Can you imagine what marriage would be like if you couldn't trust each other? All the beauty and serenity and peace of knowing that it is just you and this other person for the rest of your lives is sucked out.

A secure relationship should bring peace and stability, not jealousy. The key is to figure out what the cause is for your jealousy. Does the fault lie with him? Are you the one who is insecure? Either way, this is not a problem you can sit still on. It will not get better; it will get worse.

If you're insecure, you don't need to be—trust me. Being a Christian means that we believe God brought us into this world for a purpose. He created us and is rooting for our success. If the Creator of the universe thinks you are pretty great, that should wipe out all your insecurities.

My pastor, Dwight K. Nelson, once gave a sermon that really solidified this thought for me. It was more then just pretty words that made me feel good from a man at a pulpit. It was a meeting with destiny, and it reminded me that God only does things with a purpose.

Dictionary.com defines the word chosen as follows: "to select from a number of possibilities; pick by preference." Can we believe then, and by believe I mean truly grasp, the concept of our God, the Creator of the universe, the Center of our molecular structure, the Ultimate Designer and unparalleled Originator of Life taking the time to *choose* us? And not just choose, but by preference?

The idea for Pastor Nelson's sermon originated from the book *Ten Prayers God Always Says Yes To* written by Anthony DeStephano. The tenth prayer in the book—"God, lead me to my destiny"—was the focus of his sermon. The expansion on the topic of destiny called the congregation to ponder what kind of a God they were at church that day to serve. Our God is a systematical, methodical, precise, and meticulous God. Our God does not say oops. I had a professor once at Bethel College who used to tell my Old Testament Literature class that there is no such thing as a coincidence, only Christ-incidences. If you have faith in God, you have to put faith in His plan of creation, and in doing so you have to put faith in you.

The part of the sermon that hooked me, however, wasn't necessarily the idea of celestial routing; I already believed that. It wasn't even Pastor Nelson's compelling facts and figures; however, they did coerce me to do some research of my own. I'm not even sure that it was his opening question, "Have you ever thought about the night you were conceived," though I must say he did grab my attention. The idea that left me seeking God's affirmation and will for my life was simply the thought that when He created me, and you, He did so with a mission in mind that no other human being on the face of this earth could have accomplished.

To highlight this point, Pastor Nelson presented some facts about the mathematics of conception. You see, he explained that when you do the numbers the night you and I were conceived a single sperm had to win the race. Now, when it comes to winning the "race," it's first come first served. The first little sperm that gets there is the only sperm that finishes the race, and when that first little sperm gets there, a shield goes up and that means that 499,999,999 other little sperm have to perish. They die because the sperm that was *you* made it instead.

That's 500,000,000 other personalities. That's half a billion other possibilities, traits, and ultimately other people who could have taken your place had your single sperm, carrying your identity, not made it to your mother's egg first. And that is why DeStephano wrote that "you came into this world as a champion."

Once you let that idea marinate, you will realize that you are letting God down by not seeking His plan for your life because you were chosen by God to live. If you truly understand that, how can you ever feel insecure? Never again will there be another you. Never again, or ever before, has there ever been a person in this world exactly like you. You are an original, an original with a destiny, and that combination is what makes history.

You have a mission. A definite calling God knew no one else could fulfill. Pastor Nelson concluded this point by saying "victory was your starting point." Before you were born, you already aced your first test by winning that very important race. The idea that God chose you, by preference, should rock you to the core and also remind you that you are much more special than you sometimes think.

Hopefully that enlightenment of truth is enough to make you stop disliking yourself and start being more secure. You have to stop comparing yourself to the actresses you see in the movies, the models on the runway, or the girls in the magazine. Those girls are beautiful. They are precious to God as well, but they are no more precious to Him than you are. They are no more important in Him than you. You are equals. I think any human being worth their salt would tell you that looks really mean nothing. At some point we are all going to get old and that soft, smooth skin will get wrinkles, and those silky locks will gray. It is not the body that is precious to God, or should be to your mate, it's the soul. The Bible tells us not to worry about those who can kill the body, but instead, we should worry about those who can kill the soul.

Praise God for looking at our inward beauty and not at what is external. The world looks at what is external, labeling us as pretty or ugly, but we serve a God who created you to be beautiful. Trust me on that. And if your soul still has a plethora of blemishes, so what? You have control over that. You can fix it! You have to fix it, because you have a destiny. Remember?

If he makes you jealous, then you don't need him. Be secure in God's love, and wait for Him to bring the right guy into your life. I know this can be hard, because I often ignored the warning signs and played with fire, which caused me to get burned. Listen to your friends, trust your intuition, and talk with your parents. The people who love you can help you be strong when you feel weak.

Your parents, though terribly uncool, are actually secret bonus cards in dating. If they don't trust your boyfriend, they're probably right. I know it's hard to believe, but they once lived this dating game too. If everyone is telling you he can't be trusted, let that speak for something. You are not the smartest person in the world, and 90 percent of the time women are blinded by love. For most of us, men are our weakness. There are tons of brilliant, beautiful, inspirational women with terrible men by their sides. Men who make them feel like they aren't good enough or smart enough or pretty enough no matter what they do. Women are maternal by nature, so we are always seeing the potential that someone may have to offer, and we let that skew our vision of what's actually there. I learned, rather late in life, that potential is not enough reason to be with someone.

When you ignore everyone else's advice and then cry when things go down in flames, it really is no one else's fault but your own. Save yourself from wasting the precious moments in life. I can't tell you how many times I have wasted life by crying over someone who, in the end, I barely remember. It's a waste of emotion. Plus, if he is not the one, you are not only hurting yourself but you are hurting your lightning bolt, who is sitting around waiting for you to come along so he can strike.

He is out there! Please trust me on that. Marriage is too big a part of who you will become for God to throw up His hands and play eenie meenie miney moe. He has the perfect person just for you. The man who will make you forget all other men. He is going to be your shoulder to cry on and your hand to hold. Why are you wasting your time with someone who doesn't care enough about your precious heart to make you jealous? I'm speaking from experience.

A guy who loves you for every ounce of who you are has no need to make you feel inadequate. That person is immature. It is a problem that I think can be corrected, but he has to start loving you more than he loves himself. Loving someone else more than yourself is what true love is and you shouldn't settle for anything less.

It's common sense really. Relationships are hard. Even the happiest of couples have hard, but ultimately shaping, times. You're never going to see eye to eye on everything. You are always going to, at times, be annoyed by their presence simply because when you spend all your time with one person those sorts of things happen. That's OK. It only goes to prove that relationships are hard enough even with two people who are truly in love. To add in that mix, a guy who may make you jealous because you have adequate reason to be is a relational death sentence. In other words, jealousy almost always makes a fool of you. However, don't confuse jealousy with intuition; those are two completely separate things.

If your jealousy is actually your womanly intuition sounding off an alarm that something is not right, then you need to run, not walk, to the nearest exit. This is important because, and believe me when I tell you again, relationships are hard work. Even when everything should be right, things go wrong. If your guy makes you feel inadequate, trust me, he is not the guy for you.

Jealousy to me is a waste of emotion. That's not to say I haven't felt it. I am an extremely territorial person. But when it does come around, I try to immediately gain back my control. As far as dating a guy who would purposely make me jealous, I haven't really done it. That to me is a huge turn off. I like myself too much to be with someone who doesn't. That is probably the first step to starting a successful relationship. First, you must learn to like yourself if you don't already.

People have said it before, so I know it sounds cliché, but sometimes you can't get away from the truth. If you don't like yourself, it is going to be impossible for you to be satisfied with someone else. Either you will be way too dependent on him to give you the self-esteem you are lacking or you won't know how to let him in. This isn't going to be an easy problem to fix. The only Man I know who can fix it has probably been dying to fill you in. Pray about it. Christ is so thoughtful. Bring your worries and insecurities to Him, and let Him take control.

Just remember, with God's help you can fix yourself! As a child I was way too opinionated. I'd often interject my thoughts even when people didn't ask for my ideas. I had to learn to bite my tongue. Take it from someone who knows, nobody likes someone who thinks they know everything. I had to accept the fact that people's complaints about my personality were actually valid, and so I slowly began to change. That's not to say that I am not still opinionated. I still have strong views on several different topics, but I usually no longer voice them unless I am asked—except for my friends, they have to listen to all my thoughts, and for that, they are saints.

The main point I want to get across in this chapter is that jealousy is an age-old enemy of the human race. It's what caused Satan's fall, and it was David's jealousy of his friend's wife that led to the curse and death of his own son. In the secular world, the famous poet and writer William Shakespeare depicts jealousy in his famous work *Othello,* causing the downfall of his two characters Othello and Iago.

It almost took me an entire chapter to think of an example of jealousy in my own life, but I've thought of one tucked into the recesses of my mind. Traveling back to the fifth grade, I was madly in love—however much you can be in love in the fifth grade—with a fellow classmate. It was Valentine's Day, and I hoped with all my heart that he would give me something, anything, pledging his love for me. Well, it turned out he brought in three boxes of chocolate. He gave one to his best girlfriend and one to the teacher. I hoped the last one would be for me. I hinted around to him all day that I would love to get the box of chocolates. I complimented his outfit and told him he was so sweet for bringing chocolates for our teacher. I batted my eyes, laughed at his jokes, and then I waited for the moment of truth.

It was around lunchtime when he came up to me and handed me the box of chocolates. "Thank you so much!" I squealed with as much sincerity as was humanly possible. I showed the chocolates to every girl in the class who would give me the time of day, and I refused to eat even one of them, because I wanted to cherish this moment forever. The moment, however, was short lived. By the end of the day my crush had decided he had felt pressured into giving the chocolates to me, and though he liked me a little, he was much fonder of Katie, the blond who sat two rows in front of me. She was wearing a purple Winnie-the-Pooh T-shirt and had this pair of big blue eyes that really were something to marvel at.

Melissa, the best friend of the love of my life who had received his first box of chocolates, came up to me about five minutes before the last bell rang and asked for the chocolates back so that they could be given to Katie. My cheeks felt hot with the sting of tears, and my eyes actually burned. This was humiliating. I could have returned the chocolates. After all, I hadn't eaten any of them, and they were in perfect condition.

"Sorry, Heather," she said with much less sincerity than I had showed. After waiting for me to respond, she said, "Are you going to give them back?"

I grabbed the red heart-shaped box that probably cost a dollar and looked at them again. "No," I responded, and then I returned the box to my backpack. "Tell him I said no."

"What?" she said, looking at me as if I was pathetic. "He wants to give them to Katie, not you."

"Well, he already gave them to me," I said, and then I glanced at Katie, who was standing next to "him," waiting patiently for the return of her Valentine.

With that I took the chocolates and ran out of school. I ran the two miles home and didn't look back. When I finally got home, I ripped open my door and threw my head onto my pillow and cried. Then after about ten minutes, I got up, opened my backpack, and devoured every last one of those chocolate candies.

This story actually deals with both of my earlier topics. For one, had I not been so persistent, he probably wouldn't have given me the chocolates to begin with. It would have hurt but probably far less then having them ripped away later on. Then, as if that wasn't enough, I let jealousy make a fool of me. It would have been a much classier scenario had I handed the chocolates back, said "No problem," and smiled at Katie as she received her gift. Had jealousy not put a death grip on my emotions, I could have done that, but I didn't.

The secret weapon against jealousy is to like yourself enough to not care when someone else doesn't. If he wanted to be with Katie instead of me, so what? That just showed that we were not meant to be. And no amount of my crying or flattery would have changed that. I could have saved myself a lot of added agony if I would have realized that relationships are hard enough on their own. There is no reason to waste your time with anyone who thinks you are anything less then extraordinary.

Now, I realize that this may be a weak example because of the fact that I was probably 10, and even if he had liked me enough to pick me first, we would have broken up within a matter of weeks, but still, I hope you get my point. I think we can learn a great deal from our past. Before I close, I am going to put together a list of ways to know whether you should abandon ship and let the cards fall where they may.

It may be time to end it when:

- Your heart, your friends, and your family keep telling you that you can do better. YOU CAN!
- Eight out of 10 times he leaves the room to take his phone calls, and he never lets you see his phone. (I'm not saying you should pillage through his information daily, but if you ask him who he is texting or calling, he shouldn't have a problem telling you.) People who have nothing to hide, hide nothing.
- If you are constantly seeing flirtatious comments from other girls on his Internet accounts, something is not right. Girls do not waste their time chasing after someone who is not giving them anything back. I'm not saying break up with him, but tell him you feel uncomfortable with it, and if the flirting persists, cut your losses.
- He has a best friend of the opposite sex who he spends more time with than you. This is self-explanatory. If you were soul mates, you would be his best friend. Period.
- He barely ever makes time for you. Relationships have to be 50/50. No one is ever *too busy* to be with someone they love. If he doesn't love being with you as much as he can, you aren't the one he wants for all time, so quit wasting yours.
- He's already cheated. In my opinion, it's impossible to cheat on someone you love. The thought of hurting them would make you sick. Remember, true love is other-centered, not self-centered.
- He just isn't that nice to you. If he's verbally abusive or always makes you feel inadequate, move on. The problem's with him, not you.
- He lets his friends make fun of you. Respect is key to successful relationships. He needs to have your back at all times.
- He doesn't tell you how special you are. If he isn't somehow telling or showing you that he knows he is so lucky to have you in his life, he doesn't feel that lucky. Your soul mate will know how lucky he is to have found you, and he will find the words to let you know.

If You Guys Aren't Laughing, You're Wasting Each Other's Time

This concept is crucial, but it is often overlooked. As women we tend to put emphasis on other areas. Does he have a good job, is he attractive, do I like his family? Though I think all of those are valid in their own right, we often underestimate the power of fun. This for me is a personal revelation. I have always been a very future-orientated person. I plan everything, and I always wanted to ensure financial security for my future. That lead me to date guys who may have had a great future ahead of them, who may have been attractive, and who may have been charming, but the bottom line was that we weren't laughing.

I really noticed this one night as I was eating dinner with a long-term boyfriend of mine. We had just gotten back together after a breakup where we both saw other people. The guy I hung out with during our time apart was hilarious. Maybe it was just the combination of his personality and mine, but something was just, well, fun. When we were together, even if it was just watching TV, I was never bored. We were able to be serious when the time was right, but a lot of our time together was just spent laughing. Laughing at life, at each other, at our past. We had fun, and because of that constant sense of humor, I was happy.

Well, eventually I went back to my long-term ex-boyfriend regardless of how much fun I was having with someone else. I needed security, and I felt I had that with my ex. It was on one of our dinner dates that I realized why I was so uncertain that this person sitting across from me was my lightning bolt. We didn't laugh. In an entire dinner, we never chuckled, giggled, or even smiled. We were bored. So bored with one another's company that we were immune to each other's presence. We weren't happy, and I'm really not sure how much time had passed since we had been.

What we were was used to each other. My ex wasn't a bad boyfriend; he wasn't a loser. The problem was with *us*. The two of us together did not work. It wasn't anyone's fault; it was just the truth. Shortly after that dinner, I ended it for good. Though we ended on somewhat negative terms, I am confident that now he would agree with me. Please believe me when I say that if you aren't laughing something's not working.

Happiness is almost a synonym for laughter, and not just any kind of laughter. The best kind of laughter is the kind that forces you to put your hands over your mouth and makes your belly hurt. The kind that brings happy tears to your eyes and makes you feel complete. Life's too short to not experience those moments with your forever partner. In my opinion, it's mandatory. Life without laughter is just way too stressful, and let's face it, this world is ugly. If you want to have your glass half empty, you can find a reason to at almost every corner.

People die, money will always be tight, families will always have quarrels, and sometimes you'll be depressed. If you aren't spending every day with someone who is just so darn good at making you smile, you'll forget how to. We have enough reasons in life not to be happy. If you are married to someone who doesn't know how to lighten that load from time to time, it will just get heavier. Please believe me when I tell you it is important to place an emphasis on the way someone makes you feel. That's not to say that guys who aren't hilarious should be discarded. My point is that between the two of you there should be fun.

I am also not saying that someone who knows how to tell you a few jokes is the right person for you. Laughter, fun, and excitement are what first attracted me to my ex-fiancé. When I first met him, my mother used to tell me she knew when we were on the phone at night because every time she'd finally fall asleep she'd be woken up by my laughter. We were in a long-distance relationship, but we had so much fun together that neither of us wanted to give it up. We were addicted to this feeling of happiness we felt just by hearing each other's voice. I'd sit on the phone with him in those early days for hours and hours, and 50 percent of those conversations was honestly just pure laughter. He quickly became my best friend. I fell in love with him for his contagious personality that kept me high. I'd never been so happy. For us, however, laughter wouldn't end up being enough, and there really was nothing funny about the tragic way things ended. In life, all things need balance; you just have to find out what works for you.

This whole philosophy brings us back to the difference between a lightning bug and a lightning bolt. Bolts set you on fire. They are mesmerizing. Your soul mate will be your best friend. I can't emphasize that point enough. And they will be the person you have the most fun with.

When you are in love with your best friend, it'll be like this unbelievable secret that is locked just between you and him. You'll wonder if other people have what you have, and you'll feel sorry for them if they don't. When you're in love, you will wake up in the morning and praise God for putting you together. That's what a lightning bolt will do to you. It will strike your heart so hard that your first instinct will be to constantly praise God for bringing that kind of power into your life. You'll never get tired of thanking Him. And remember, if it's meant to be and you seek God's will and truly allow Him full reign, He will answer you. Just be prepared that His answer may be completely different than what you think is your destiny. That's because He can see the end from the beginning. God sees the whole picture while our thinking can only cover the past and the present. Trust Him completely, and He will not take something away without eventually giving you something better.

Love is laughing at the quirks in someone and loving them for it. Love is missing someone right when they are gone. When you realize you want to spend the rest of your life with somebody, you want the rest of your life to start as soon as possible.

In order to prove my theory of the importance of laughter, I did some research. I read several articles, one of which was a piece that provided lots of information on the health benefits of laughing. Apparently laughter is not only great for your life but it is great for your body. It improves breathing, lowers blood pressure, strengthens the immune system, relaxes muscles, releases stress, and reduces pain. Laughter even releases natural killer cells that assist your body in fighting off colds and viruses. I think God knew that not only would being with someone who makes you laugh be good for your heart but that it would be essential in keeping you physically healthy. The only prescription necessary is to find the person who gives you lots of it and with whom you can share it.

I have a very dear friend who has been in a relationship with her on-again-off-again boyfriend for about seven or so years now. We had dinner together one day and giggled like schoolgirls.

"See, this is what I miss about hanging out with my girlfriends," she said. "I miss laughing."

I was surprised to hear her say she missed laughing. In the relationship I was in at the time, laughter was largely a part of our fun. He made me smile when I took situations or myself too seriously. Even though things didn't work out for us, I wouldn't trade some of the good things that that relationship taught me. I remember what life was like pre-laughter, and I wouldn't go back for anything. Of course, I told her that if she wasn't having fun with him there was obviously a problem. Not to mention their breakup rate increased at the speed of light. But we'll talk about that later.

Laughter is probably the one aspect of that relationship that changed me forever—it was the one aspect that we actually got right. In my own life, I can't tell you how priceless it was to be with someone who made me smile. I remember one time when I was crying my eyes out. I really don't even remember what had happened; I just know I was sitting on the couch next to him, and I was emptying my soul of every tear it ever held. It was before we were even officially together, and I usually don't cry in front of people, but whatever had happened had caused me to lose my control.

He sat there and tried to console me. He held my hand and told me it was going to be OK. I could barely see him through my blurry vision, and I wrinkled my face and let the tears continue to roll.

"Please don't cry," he said, probably unsure of what else to say. "I'm worried that if you don't stop you won't have any water left in you, and you'll turn into a prune."

It wasn't even that funny, but I couldn't believe he had said it. I wiped my eyes for a moment and looked at him again. He had a nervous grin on his face as if he wasn't sure how I would respond. Before I knew it, I was laughing—half laughing and half groaning because my vocal chords weren't ready for the sudden switch in emotions. He leaned over and kissed me on my forehead, and my face grew hot to his touch.

"You're prettier when you aren't crying," he said as I took a tissue and wiped all the snot from my nose. "Much prettier." He smiled in a way that told me he was kidding, but still, I thought I might love him, and so I tried never to cry again.

Now there is an opposite side to this. I shouldn't even have to get into this, but some people need things spelled out, and I don't want any of you to miss out on this. When I am talking about laughter, I am referring to it within the realms of love. All your humor should be clean. If the only times you laugh are when you are making fun of other people, the two of you are shallower than a kiddie pool.

I carry a genuine chip on my shoulder against people who make fun of other people because it makes them feel better about themselves. I hate mean people because I used to be one of them. If your heart is ugly and you treat other people like they are lower than you rather then equal to you, I don't think you know God, because God is love, and His love includes everyone. As a pre-teen, I was awful. I bullied people and made girls cry. I can't offer an explanation as to why I did it, but I did, and I've felt guilty ever since. At some point, however, I'd like to think that even bullies grow up. At least I did. I met a God who loved unconditionally, and it moved me. I instantly fell in love with the idea of love, and I let it change me. If you truly know Christ, people should be able to tell. If you want to pray to God for guidance, I suggest you make an effort to make sure there isn't anything that could be hindering your prayers. Hate is definitely a hindrance.

Looking at laughter again, you need balance. Too many jokes, gag gifts, tricks, or witty remarks could be a cover up for a lack of substance. Humor should never be malicious or mean spirited. Making jokes about each other's weaknesses or physical insecurities is not funny. Neither of you should be the butt of each other's jokes, in front of your friends or just with each other.

When I say I want you to laugh, I also mean I want you to enjoy each other's company. In order to enjoy each other's company, you have to sincerely know the other person and let them know you. Neither of you can do that if you are never taking each other seriously. Possibly the best aspect of love is that there is someone out there who knows everything about you—every ambition, desire, or shortcoming, every positive or negative trait. Relationships need to be full of laughter but at the same time be filled with down-to-earth, real conversations. If you aren't experiencing any of that, end it.

I don't mean to be cold when I suggest you bite the bullet and end the relationship, but I just don't see the value of wasting your time. Usually, if you have any actual doubts, there is good reason for it. I know people always say that when you meet the right one "you just know it." I had two really serious long-term boyfriends in my life and one fiancé who I loved to death. I thought I would marry each of them.

I dedicated about three years apiece to each relationship, and I was sure that each time was different. I was uneasy though because that line always bothered me: "You'll just know." I always heard it reverberating in my ears, but I never "knew it." I wanted, I hoped, I worked hard, and I prayed, but I never felt certain. Now, these guys were wonderful, and I don't mean to diminish the time I spent getting to know them, but I do wish I had taken my uncertainty as a sign. I should have let them go and let them find the girls they belonged with. Instead, I wasted nine years of my life.

I was the girl who always had a boyfriend. I had a few really close girlfriends, but I would ditch them in a New-York minute to spend time with my boyfriend. I lost out on a lot of good relationships throughout high school and college because I was "that girl" who always got a boyfriend and suddenly was struck with tunnel vision. I missed out on an entire four years of high school—I missed trips, and dinners, and movies—because I was spending all my available time with lightning bugs. They were great people, but it was simply not meant to be, and I probably would have known that sooner if I weren't putting what I wanted before what God was telling me.

I wish now that I would have seen the signs and just waited for Mr. Right to come along. I guess the good thing is that now I have, and there is no time for change like the present. If I wouldn't have been so distracted, I can honestly tell you that I would have waited my entire life to date and just spent my time with friends until that right person came along. If I had paid more attention to the lack of response from my prayers, I would have realized that that lack of response was my answer. I used to beg God to just let me have that feeling. Let me know for certain that this person was the one for me, and He was silent, and I ignored it. I said it earlier, but that's another thing about prayer. If you ask God for something, be ready to act upon His answer.

As I close this chapter, I want to point out something I have yet to say. It is your duty to make your boyfriend feel just as special and loved and adored as you want him to make you feel. You need to be making him smile every day, too. You need to compliment him on his good points and not spend all your time nagging his flaws. Build him up and make sure every single day he is absolutely positive that you love him.

I think that is a big mistake some women make—they think everything is all about them. Relationships need to be balanced. Love should be distributed evenly. If you are not making him feel loved, there is someone else who will. Likewise if he is not doing his part to ensure your happiness, there is another man who can fill his shoes. Relationships don't work without sacrifice. You must, even when you don't want to, tell him you're sorry or that you forgive him. If he is truly your lightning bolt, treat him like the rare and precious treasure he is. Love him with every ounce of love you have.

If It Didn't Work the Last Three Times, This Time Won't Be Different

It was beautiful while it lasted, but it's pretty shabby now. It's the cycle of the exes. We all have had them. That one relationship that never seemed to end, but end it must. There are several reasons why a relationship that has ended must actually be over. For one, the average guy isn't going to be attracted to baggage, and that's exactly what you've got if you are holding on to an off-again-on-again ex-boyfriend. You're basically wearing a sign that says, "I'm single, but I'm not." Move on, so that you can find your lightning bolt.

Trust me on this one; I've lived it. This is a chapter that could be lengthened into a book. I don't know what it is about long-term relationships, but for some reason we just can't let them die peacefully. We have to keep digging them back up, searching the casket for any remains we think can be salvaged. Put down the shovel and walk away slowly. There's no pulse left; if there was you wouldn't have put it six feet under in the first place.

First of all, I am not talking about people who are in a long-term relationship and break up once and get back together. I think breaking up once can happen to any couple, especially if they started dating young. (By young I mean dating in high school or during their freshmen year of college.) During those years you are still finding yourself, figuring out just what it is you want out of life, and it isn't strange for people to get confused and break up with someone only to realize that it was a terrible mistake. But listen carefully, I said breakup ONCE! Not the three- to eight-time breakup cycles other girls, including myself, have gotten caught in. By then, no one is taking this relationship seriously, not even the two of you.

If you can say goodbye to him more than once, he is not your soul mate, and vice versa. If you break up because you feel as though the flame has died, or you meet someone more intriguing, or you want to see what else is out there, stay broken up. If he was the one, you would have never let him go, not even for a second. If he has dumped you more than once, tell him bon voyage. Just like us, guys can get caught up in this sense of security. The fact that he knows you will always be there for him is usually appealing. Because of this he will come back to you after he rips your heart to pieces because he misses being loved, not necessarily because he loves you. All you are is a big safety net that he can fall on when he gets lonely and needs to be reminded that someone cares. You deserve to be someone's lifeline.

Real love doesn't come and go, and come and go, and come and go. It stays. It says, "Life without this person is unthinkable." I should also note here that if a fight about whether to go to Taco Bell or McDonald's quickly escalades into an "I-hate-you-I-never-want-to-talk-to-you-again" brawl, it's safe to say it's over. A girl I worked with once told me that if you dump someone, it's because you think there is something better, and if you go back to that same person, it's because you are worried you won't find it. If this is true, and I think it's plausible considering human nature, then breakups should really be just that—a quick ending to a relationship that just wasn't working. Trust me, when you are with the right person, you won't even think about what else could be out there. You'll be too busy praising God you found who you did.

Now, on to my story. I broke up with my first serious boyfriend twice, and that was it. The second time we knew it was over, and there was no long, exaggerated ending. We'd been together for three years, but we broke up on good terms and wished each other the best. My second relationship, however, didn't end so easy. We broke up, and broke up, and broke up. I cannot even tell you how many times we probably broke up and got back together. We broke up for a day, we broke up for a week, for a month, and I think the longest was probably about three or four months before we, of course, got back together, only to break up for good.

It wasn't healthy, and no matter how much time we spent apart it didn't change the fact that we were simply mismatched. When things finally did end, it was worse than it would have been had we just walked away the first time. He did things he probably wouldn't have done had the relationship not gotten so incredibly unhealthy, and I did things I still hate myself for. You see, we both started out as good people, but the longer we stayed in the agonizing cycle we changed. I think it made us both a little crazy.

To this day I blame myself for not ending things when I knew it was over. Because of my selfishness and the fact that I was scared to be alone, I dragged him on this roller coaster that seemed to only go down hills. I don't want to dwell on this too much as an example, but I really did learn so much about myself from that experience. I learned a lot about the importance of honesty in a relationship. Honesty really is the core in what keeps people accountable to themselves and God. I really think that anyone would rather have you be honest, even if what you say hurts, than have you lie.

I also think that far too often we look at breakups as failures. We stay in terrible relationships because we don't want an awful stain on our tract record. You spend a lot of time building a relationship with someone, and to watch it die after all the time and care you put into it can be a hard thing to do. It takes a large level of maturity to realize when something isn't working and simply walk away. I don't want you to think I don't understand how hard it is to go through a breakup; whether you're 14 or 41, breaking up is always painful. As women, when we grow up and get married and have children one of the biggest thoughts we have when looking at that perfect beautiful baby girl in our arms is, how do I comfort this angel when someone breaks her heart? How, as her mother, can I look her in the eyes when she thinks her world is absolutely over and assure her that it's not?

I'm not sure there is a perfect way to help someone through something like that. I was so devastated with my first breakup that I couldn't even bring myself to go to school, and I was the one that ended it with him! It didn't matter who ended it; the point was that it was over and it killed me. I was a senior in high school, and I got in my car and just drove. I passed trees and houses and people, and I looked at the vastness of the sky and cried. I prayed to God to help get me through, and I choked on tears as I drove to the only tangible person I thought might understand. I pulled into the parking lot where my mother worked, and with tears in my eyes, I walked past the secretary and into her office. When she saw me, she rose from her desk and quickly went to shut the door.

"What's wrong?" she asked as she put her hand on my shoulder.

It was over. It had been over for a few days, but the tears just didn't seem to have a stopping point.

"I miss him," I answered through gasps of breath. I can't tell you verbatim what she said, but I remember it was something about her first boyfriend and how she thought she'd never move on when they ended but how glad she was that they had because she met my dad.

I don't know what it is when you're a kid, but for some reason we assume our parents never had a life outside of us and our family. I had never even considered that my mother may have dated someone else. I tried to comprehend what my mother was saying and accept the fact that the right person was still out there and if I was patient enough, He'd bring him to me. Even after all I have been through, I am pretty confident that one day God will give me a daughter who will of course think that I never had any dating problems. She will think that I was born and met her dad in the nursery and that things just progressed smoothly from there. My point is that eventually—though it's hard to see while you are still in the thick of it—none of this will matter.

My mother was right that day. She said I'd move on, and I did. She said it was going to be OK, that God was in control, and that I didn't have to worry. I stopped crying and sat with her for a few more minutes before forcing myself to go back to school, to move on. I think I cried again that night, and then some the next day, but each day it got less and less, until the tears found a stopping point.

No matter what, you have to be honest with yourself and with the other person. In some of my relationships I felt as though I had to stick around for him because it would reflect poorly on me to break his heart. I knew everyone would talk about me and make me out to be this wicked woman simply because I wasn't happy anymore. At some point, however, you have to come to grips with the fact that you can't live life for anyone but yourself. Sometimes you will do things with perfectly good intentions and people will still hate you for it. The best advice one of my professors gave me was that you can't make everyone happy. If you are seeking God's leading and staying in tune with your heart, you will make the right decision, even if other people don't think so.

Regardless of who initiates the breakup, it will be hard. I'd like to tell you that you will both be able to move on and remain friends, but most of the time you won't. In most instances, someone gets hurt, but in the grand scheme of things, breaking up is far better than living a lie. You will begin to resent each other if you try to force a relationship. Honesty really is the best policy.

There is another problem we should discuss when dealing with ex-boyfriends and that is how you can be a "good" ex. Let's face it; even the best of girls can turn into evil-spewing demons when dumped. Stay classy. If you run around town talking bad about him, it's going to backfire, because you're going to be the one who is deemed crazy, which for most guys is a complete turn off.

I know it can be hard to separate painful feelings from rational logic, so here are a few things to remember. It is never logical to post your despair or his shortcomings on Facebook, slash his tires, or scream at him in public. Trust me; you are not getting back at him. All you are doing is solidifying in his mind that he was completely right in breaking it off with you, because you are nuts. You are also scaring off future suitors who watch your tirade.

What you do need to do is to remain calm and cool. It's OK to cry, but do it when you're alone or with your parents. It's OK to be emotional, but try to stay away from the reminders that make you cry or incite rage. It's probably necessary to delete him from all your Internet communities so you don't spend all your time staring at his pictures or driving yourself crazy wondering who he is talking to. Feel free to burn his photos, give back his things, and pretend he never existed. It is important to realize that he is the one who is missing out here, and once you truly allow yourself to believe that things will be OK it will get a lot easier. Remember, if it doesn't work out, it's because God didn't want it to. There is someone else, someone better, and the quicker you get over your ex the better off you will be.

The next aspect to being an ex-girlfriend comes into play when you are the one who did the dumping. Please do not be the type of girl who breaks his heart and then wants him back again the second you find out he has a new girlfriend. It's not nice to steal other girls' boyfriends, even if he was "yours" in the first place. I think almost all ex-girlfriends, including myself, have been "that girl" at some point.

I had been over my ex-boyfriend for months, but one day I logged onto Facebook and saw that he was in a relationship with someone else. "Wait a second," I thought, "you mean he is not sitting there, months later, still mulling over me? How dare he move on?" Before I knew it my fingers were flying on the keyboard, drafting a private message in hopes of luring him away from her. Of course, it worked. We had history. She was unfairly equipped to go to war with me because, after all, I was the ex-girlfriend. I destroyed their budding relationship in a matter of days only to add to our long list of breakups. It was wrong, and I feel terrible about it now. People can't be disposable. You can't degrade them like I did. Be better than me.

On the same note, if you are the one in the budding relationship and you notice the ex-girlfriend is still lingering around, immediately tell him that it is either her or you. If your guy is truly over her, the decision won't be hard. Trust me on this; no matter how much prettier, smarter, or funnier you are compared to her you cannot underestimate the power of the ex-girlfriend. There was something about her that attracted him to her in the first place, even if you don't see it. If he is taking his relationship with you seriously, he will cut her off completely.

The truth is, however, that it is usually us women who are the ones being lured. It seems like guys have a sixth sense—the second they know you may be actually getting over them they swoop in out of nowhere and declare to have figured everything out. Don't be swayed by his constant phone calls, impromptu visits, or declarations of change. If you've met someone else, don't ruin it over someone who has already decided he is better off without you. Think about it; he actually sat and thought and came to the conclusion that his life would be better lived if you weren't in it. What about that should keep you wishing he'd come back?

So many of our dating problems would be solved if we, as women, simply realized how great we are. Sure, we may not have fit great with him, but that is simply that match. It doesn't mean anything more than that. It just means that the two of you didn't work out. Nothing is wrong with you. Don't miss out on the "right" one because you are trying to board a ship that has already sunk.

The last thing I think should be mentioned in this saga of the exes is the age-old question "should we stay friends?" In my opinion, and that's all this is, you shouldn't. Not friends in the sense where you still hang out and call each other. That route is not at all helpful if you are trying to move on. Someone once told me that if two people can break up and remain friends they were either never in love or still are. I find that statement to be extremely wise, and since hearing it, I have measured all my ended relationships by it.

Sometimes there are guys who you date where you quickly realize you were better off as friends. In that case, you never were actually in love, so it is probably safe to stay in touch. But if he was your entire world for years, you have no choice but to bid him farewell. It will only cause problems in your future relationships if you keep him around. Your new boyfriend shouldn't have to worry about whether or not there is still something there, even if there isn't. If you won't terminate your friendship with your ex-boyfriend for your new boyfriend, you probably shouldn't be dating anyone. You still need more time to figure out exactly what it is you want.

I really think we underestimate the role Christ should play in our relationships. We put Him on the back burner and then are surprised when we get burned. God needs to be the Pilot of your relationships. He needs to be included when you make decisions and consulted when you make mistakes. It took me 23 years to learn how to value Christ's opinion and to take it as the final authority. In the Bible God specifically gave Rebekah to Isaac. Before Isaac even knew who she was, God had chosen her for him.

Abraham (Isaac's father) didn't want Isaac to take a wife from Canaan. He wanted a woman who would uphold the family's covenant with God, so he sent his faithful servant to travel 500 miles toward Abraham's homeland of Nahor. The servant took 10 camels with him on this long journey. Upon reaching his destination, he stopped at a well to pray to God to send him the right woman whom he could bring back to marry Isaac, Abraham's son.

The story is recorded in Genesis 24:42-48: "When I came to the spring today, I said, 'LORD, God of my master Abraham, if you will, please grant success to the journey on which I have come. See, I am standing beside this spring. If a young woman comes out to draw water and I say to her, "Please let me drink a little water from your jar," and if she says to me, "Drink, and I'll draw water for your camels too," let her be the one the Lord has chosen for my master's son.'

"Before I finished praying in my heart, Rebekah came out, with her jar on her shoulder. She went down to the spring and drew water, and I said to her, 'Please give me a drink.' She quickly lowered her jar from her shoulder and said, 'Drink, and I'll water your camels too.' So I drank, and she watered the camels also.

"I asked her, 'Whose daughter are you?'

"She said, 'The daughter of Bethuel son of Nahor, whom Milkah bore to him.'

"Then I put the ring in her nose and the bracelets on her arms, and I bowed down and worshiped the Lord."

God cares about who you will spend the rest of your life with. He cared about Isaac and Rebekah, and He cares about you. Just trust Him, and wait with patience for His answers, because He will answer, even if through the silence He tells you that His answer is no.

If Your Net Catches a Lightning Bug, Set Him Free

When I was a kid, probably 6 or 7, my absolute favorite summer activity was catching lightning bugs. That's probably a dead giveaway that I grew up in the Midwest, with not much to do but jump rope and play hopscotch, but catching lightning bugs was my idea of a good time. My parents even bought me a net so I could run around outside in the dark and with ease snatch my next little friend. I can still feel the warm summer air and see the pitch-black sky with its bursts of brightness, which I called "stars."

I loved the lightning bugs because they were like tiny little stars flying around in the air. They were tricky because one second I would see the neon glow of their bright little bulb, and the next second they would vanish. I'd lift my net and trap them as quickly as I could. Sometimes I'd collect 10 of them, others only one. Then I'd take my precious little bugs and put them in a jar with holes in the lid so they could breathe, and I'd simply watch them. The sad thing is that lightning bugs really don't live that long. Looking back, it was terrible that I'd trap the little creatures and force them to live out the rest of their days in captivity. All they were was a centerpiece—something I could look at inside the jar. However, every once in awhile I would feel some compassion for the creatures and set them free.

OK, so you may not be handcuffing your boyfriend to your dresser and forcing him to follow you around. You may not have placed him in a tiny jar with a few air holes simply for your amusement. You may not have strung a net to catch him, but you are wasting his time. Set him free; tell him the truth. You don't have to be cruel and tell him that you want nothing to do with him, but you should not hold on to something that isn't there.

Now, this captive may or may not be your ex-boyfriend. He may just be the guy who you keep around just in case all else fails. The only problem is this: if he's back-burner material, he will never warm your heart. Not in the way true love does. The best thing you can do is to let him find his real sweetheart. Just because he's not your bolt, doesn't mean he's not someone else's.

I am not going to name any names, but I have seen personal friends of mine be extremely guilty of this. I've seen them hoarding four or five guys at a time just in case they start to feel lonely. It's not right, ladies. You wouldn't want someone leading you on, so why do you think it's right to do it to someone else? As Christians we should treat others how we would like to be treated, and this definitely applies to dating.

I think the guys who usually get placed into our "jars" are our best friends. That one guy who we think knows us best and always seems to make us feel better when he's around. In my opinion, this guy could actually be the soul mate you are looking for, but only you can know that. I've had best guy friends who I secretly adored, and best guy friends who were just that, friends. If the chemistry is there, let him know and pursue it, but if not, you really need to make sure he knows exactly where you stand. It just isn't fair for him to be missing out on a really great girl because you're sending him signals that you're interested when you really aren't.

From eighth grade through high school, I had a best guy friend. We'll call him Brock. Brock and I did everything together, and not only were we best of friends but the entire school knew it. During Christmastime it was our tradition to go driving on a Friday night and look at everyone's Christmas lights. On half days of school, I'd go to his house, and we'd make macaroni and cheese and watch TV. I absolutely adored his family. I'd often call his mother and tell her what was currently going on in my life, and she, in turn, would invite me over for family dinners and root beer floats.

His mother always hinted to me that she thought we should be together, and I couldn't have agreed with her more. It was Brock who was clueless. Looking back, I can probably assume he wasn't clueless at all. He knew exactly what he was doing. It wasn't until I got a boyfriend that he started to get antsy. He'd tell me that he realized he had feelings for me and that he was just nervous because we were "such good friends."

That should have been my caution sign right there. Listen to me closely when I say this, there are absolutely zero men out there who are actually worried about ruining your friendship. If a guy likes you enough, he is going to make sure you know it. The majority of men are hunters by nature. They see what they want, and they love trying to get it. Most people live in the here and now, and thinking about future problems is extremely rare. If a guy tells you that he is worried about ruining your friendship, he is politely letting you down. He is nicely telling you that although he may have a crush on you it is nothing he feels about strongly enough to pursue. Take his gentle hints, and trudge on.

Anyway, Brock was killing me softly. He was dedicating songs to me, making me Valentines out of construction paper during art class, and writing me precious little notes. He asked me to the winter formal, one of my high school dances, and he said that he felt we should explore our relationship romantically. Brock was lying. Well, perhaps not in the vindictive sense of the word, but he knew he wasn't actually ever going to give me what I wanted. He was never going to settle down with just me and allow me the satisfaction of telling his mom. He was, however, nervous I wouldn't be around anymore, and so he did whatever necessary to keep me reeling. I'm not saying I loved Brock, but it was torture to be his "friend" for the next four years. It was agonizing to think that just maybe he may decide he felt for me the way I felt for him. What was worse was that he gave me all the signs that he did. He bought a front row ticket to my pageant, saved me a seat in class, called me on Saturday nights to get something to eat, and made sure his mother picked me up for every single one of his football games.

I'm still not sure why he wouldn't just be with me. I couldn't force him though, and I spent the next four years in that same status quo with him. Even when I dated other people, I always secretly hoped he would come around. As long as he wasn't sending me mixed signals, I could move on. Eventually I had to cut him off. By the time our senior year came around, he was back at his old ways and I was single again. I thought surely this time was going to be it. I prayed about him often because I was very convinced that he was the one for me. Well, much to my dismay, and I think to his mother's, he started dating a girl from another town, and he stayed with her for the entire year. I was devastated at first, and then I decided it was typical and I should have seen it coming.

By graduation I rarely saw him, and we were both in serious relationships so I just let it go. It wasn't until my freshmen year of college that Brock finally saw what I had seen all along. Almost out of the blue he called me and asked if we could see a movie or have dinner— "Anything that lets us talk," he said. He had broken up with his girl-friend a month or so ago and couldn't believe we barely knew each other anymore. I had almost forgotten about him. I was in a new place with new friends, and I honestly wasn't thinking at all about who I was in high school. For old time's sake, I decided to go. Everything was just like it used to be except this time before he dropped me off he told me he thought he was in love with me. It was different this time. I could tell he meant it. He continued to tell me how stupid he had been before and how he didn't know why he never realized this in high school. He told me I was beautiful, inside and out, and he reminded me how much I loved his family.

"Can you imagine us together?" he said smiling. "It would be so perfect. So easy."

Strangely enough, my sister had actually just called me the week before and asked if I ever talked to Brock anymore. "I have a feeling you guys will end up together," she said, very certain of herself.

As I sat there in his red sports car, staring into his deep blue eyes and watching his lips as he spoke, I was very touched. This is what I had wanted since the eighth grade. I had always been the best friend and never the girlfriend. When he had dated my best friend, even though it only lastcd a month of two, it had killed me. It was so easy for him to be in a relationship with everyone else but me.

During our senior year in speech class we had to give speeches on important people in our lives. He wrote about me, and I wrote about him. I remember I purposely made my speech comical, hoping no one would see through me and see how serious I really was about him. He came late the day I gave mine, so he never did hear it. The last line in my speech was something like this: "Though he can drive me crazy, I wouldn't trade Brock for anything. He's my best friend, and I love him." I remember that when he gave his speech, without ever hearing mine, the last line was almost identical to mine. "I wouldn't trade Heathcr for anything," he said, his face starting to turn a little red as I sat in the second to front row in front of the desk where he sat. "Even if she does kick me with her pointy heels and her big head blocks the blackboard so I can't take notes." Everyone laughed, and he smiled and winked at me before he sat down.

All of these images came to my mind right before I said, "Kiss me."

Throughout the years, we had kissed each other a few times, and I had always gotten goose bumps and butterflies in my stomach. Back then I would have died had he said everything he was saying to me now. I would have told him to hold on so I could have called his mother and told her I was going to be her daughter-in-law. I would have called my sister and all my best friends and told them that he had finally seen me.

As we leaned toward each other in his car, I closed my eyes and held my breath. This was it; it was really happening. As we pulled apart, I opened my eyes. His mouth was curled into a cute half grin, and he was blushing.

"What do you think?" he asked, reaching for my hand.

"I think . . . I think that we should just be friends," I answered him, and I knew he knew I meant it. I felt nothing when he kissed me. No sparks, no butterflies, and definitely no goose bumps. He put the car in gear and drove me to my dorm.

As we said goodbye, I said, "For so long this is exactly what I wanted, and now I just don't have any of those feelings anymore. I had to get over you, and I guess you are just too late now."

I wasn't being mean, and he knew I wasn't. I was being honest. I guess all the games he had played in high school had at some point left me numb to him. I wasn't mad at him for the past, and I wasn't trying to get back at him. I just was at a different place in my life. It was funny too, because before I had always thought that I would always have feelings for him. At some point though while I was praying to God to make him see me the way I saw him, God changed me. I wasn't the same girl in high school, beaming because he saved me a seat. I had met tons of new guys, and I had learned a lot about myself. I was different now, and in my eyes, so was he.

I don't hold any resentful feelings toward Brock. All's well that ends well, right? I am cognizant, however, that what Brock did was wrong, and if I can prevent someone doing it to someone else, then maybe it was all worth it. If you know someone is never going to be more than your friend, please let them go. Hook them up with one of your friends, be honest with them every step of the way, and let them fly.

On the other hand, I also take responsibility for my actions. If you are not the one doing the capturing but are the tiny bug stuck in someone else's jar, there is nothing wrong with setting yourself free. Like I said before, and this is probably the most important point in this entire book, you have to start realizing that you are valuable. Once you let that thought sink in, you have no choice but to leave the jar and go in search of someone who will treasure you for the person you are.

Remember, you were created and chosen by Christ Himself to enter this world. You have a mission, and the person you marry will be part of it. That construction is too important for God to ignore. If you ask Him, He will be a part of every decision you have to make—whether it is dealing with your family, your job, or who you are dating. You are special. You deserve so much, and each person is entitled to be treated with respect and dignity.

In Matthew 22:36–40 a teacher who was wise in the law asked Jesus what the most important commandment was: "'Teacher, which is the greatest commandment in the Law?' Jesus replied: 'Love the Lord your God with all your heart and with all your soul and with all your mind.' This is the first and greatest commandment. And the second is like it: 'Love your neighbor as yourself.' All the Law and the Prophets hang on these two commandments."

Once we truly begin to love one another for who we are, we will also learn to truly appreciate each other's worth. No one was created to sit idly in your glass jar, and you should not sit in anyone else's. Treat everyone the way you would like them to treat you. Love each other as you would love yourself. Not only will this make you better off in finding your lightning bolt, but it will also make you a better Christian, a better example.

Also, it's important to be sure that you aren't so consumed in finding your soul mate that you leave no time for God. God should always be your number one priority. If you are worried you aren't going to meet anyone, spend some more of your free time reading the Bible and building a better understanding of who God is. This will only make you a better fit for your mate when Christ brings him into your life.

Oftentimes one of Satan's biggest war tactics is to simply keep us so busy in the routines of everyday life that we forget to spend time with God. Satan is a genius in the art of deception. He knows that the things you are spending all of your time doing don't even have to be bad—it can be something as simple as searching the Internet, watching TV, reading, listening to music, or spending time with friends. By themselves these things can be harmless, but when you allow yourself to become consumed, they are lethal. You see, all Satan needs is for you to just keep knocking God down on your list of priorities.

I really think the key to relational and personal happiness is linked to relationships with Christ. He is much more apt to give you the last piece of your puzzle when you are in a good, grounded place with Him. He will not give you anything you are not ready for, and the best way to get ready is to stay close to Him. America is drowning in a sea of single-parent families and high divorce rates because people are not including God in every aspect of their lives. When will we realize that Jesus Christ is the key to every trace of possible human happiness? Knowing Him will make every morsel of goodness better and every crumb of evil insignificant. Once you begin to understand who He is, you will also know that He says we can ask Him for anything. Remember, God says that anything we ask for in accordance with His will, will be met. What could be more in accordance with His will than you seeking out His partner for your life? Test Him on this. He is the Best Friend, Father, and Lord you will ever serve. Take Him at His word. I did, and I will never go back. I couldn't go back. Jesus set me free.

R-E-S-P-E-C-T: Respect

Respect. This seven-letter word is a crucial factor in all relationships. It should be given freely because love is there. It does not work unless it is given both ways, and without it whatever you are trying to work out will be impossible. If he is the one, he will respect your heart, your body, and your mind. You will be his number one priority, and when someone else hurts you, it will hurt him. These seven simple letters are vital to your survival.

Growing up, my father always told us that all you really have is family and if someone tries to mar or hurt any person within that family circle you must defend them. I never forgot this. That is why in every relationship I have ever had, even though things may not have been perfect, I made crystal clear the importance the role of respect would play.

I remember one time when I first started hanging out with one of my exes. I knew things were going to get serious because he asked me what the most important things were to me in a relationship. His exact words were something like this: "What are the three things that, if they weren't there, would be a deal breaker in a relationship?"

My answer almost came without thinking because I have always been into making lists and planning ahead for exactly what it was I wanted in and out of another person. I think for women especially it is important to make a list of the attributes you cannot live without, a list of things that would be a plus or a bonus, and then things that you know you absolutely would never want in someone. This can be important because if you make it when you're clearheaded and not blinded by love, it can be a really good thing to come back to later when things are getting kind of foggy.

Oftentimes, although we have a list, when we meet someone who is really cute, we throw out one or two of the things we once thought to be vital. We say, "So what if he doesn't believe in God right now, I can change him," or "So he doesn't have a job, is extremely lazy, and freeloads off his parents, he'll grow up." Trust me, 99 percent of the time you are not going to change him. People are who they are. If you can't accept him for who he is today, then you really need to move on.

I am probably the number one offender of constantly trying to change the person I'm with. I had to learn the hard way that it's really rare for people to change and impossible when it's not for themselves. If he is changing simply to be with you, eventually that need to please you will die off and he will wonder why you can't just accept him for who he is. The truth is that he is right. If you can't accept him for who he is right at that moment, then move on.

I will admit that there are a small percentage of men who will meet that one girl who just snaps them out of their bad habits, and for her, he is a new man. But please, don't assume you are that girl. In fact, assume you're not. Every girl wants to be "that girl," yet almost every girl isn't. The problem with women is that we all think we are somehow better than everyone else. We are all so positive of our own uniqueness. I don't want to be harsh or burst any bubbles, but most of us are actually very similar. That's why Hollywood can market a whole slew of movies and books to fit our gender, and we all take it in. The truth is that although we may vary in values, beliefs, and opinions the core thoughts of a woman are usually one in the same.

That is not a bad thing. God created us like that because we are one side of what His personality is like. He made us in His image, and that image represents His caring and loving side. He made us different from man because we are man's other complimentary half. We are usually everything that a man is not, and he is everything we are not, and together we can make up everything that Christ is.

At any rate, going back to the story where I was asked what I needed in a relationship, I told him my three relationship criteria: first and foremost, he must be a Christian; second, my family had to approve; and third, he had to respect me.

"What do you mean by respect you?" he questioned. He wanted it spelled out.

To me, when someone respects you they not only value you but they have your best interest at heart. You can take what they say at face value because there are no concealed motives or manipulation tactics. I wanted someone who respected me and heard my thoughts and ideas, someone who cherished my opinion whether they personally agreed with it or not. I wanted someone whom I could make a family with. Someone I could trust to always have my back. Someone who would respect me enough to keep personal things within our relationship private, and someone who would respect my body as much as my mind.

"I think I can do that," he said, winking at me.

My list of things I need may be different from yours, and that's fine. We all have different personalities with different needs, but I really encourage you to place respect on your list. If you do nothing else, find a man who respects you. I cannot relay to you enough how much it really kills me to see women settle for men who degrade them. That type of relationship does not get better; it only gets worse. Young women in today's society are saturated by MTV, negative rap music, and reality television so much so that we are almost unaware of what the word respect even means. Everywhere you look on television, in the movies, and in magazines you find scantily dressed women vying for male attention. Unfortunately it isn't just in the media where we see this phenomenon. Our society is adapting to this new mindset that in order to get attention from the opposite sex, you have to flaunt your body and degrade yourself.

The fact that 13-year-old girls are taking photos of themselves naked and sending it to their crush via text message shows that we've lost all concepts of morality and respect. Although I never took pictures of myself naked, I did dress scantily in order to attract attention. Before I truly gave myself to Christ, I went along with the idea that I was a sex object. I went to Halloween parties basically wearing nothing but my underpants. I wanted men to think I was sexy. I lived for the affirmation of a room full of guys all trying to make their way over to where I was standing.

Now that I have matured past that ridiculous behavior, I want to spare others from the pain and humiliation I went through. It makes me sad to see my friends post revealing pictures of themselves online for a group of "friends" to see—most of whom they don't even know. They do it, and I did it, just to be reminded that they are pretty. It's all so absurd when I think of it now. As women we have struggled for years to smash the glass ceiling and be taken seriously, but we are now going backward, posing for a camera hoping people, especially men, will still think we are pretty. It's crazy when you think about it.

I say all this because I think it is hard to find someone who truly respects you if you are not respecting yourself. I'm not saying that there is anything wrong with wanting to be attractive, but taking your clothes off to do it is not the solution.

If you want to be beautiful, let it shine from the inside out—that will amaze people. I'm telling you all this in hopes that you will learn from my mistakes. If it were not for the forgiveness and mercy of God, I don't know where I would be right now. Women have so many amazing qualities. I'm not saying you can't be proud of your looks or style; I'm just saying you should be able to impress people with more than just that. Looks fade, but your character and reputation last forever.

I have learned that guys who are actually looking for the woman they want to spend the rest of their lives with usually don't find them half naked at a party. When I chose to leave the party scene, I met lots of people and had some of the best conversations of my life. All of a sudden I had guys wanting to talk to me! And they weren't just saying rehearsed lines that they would be using the next day on another girl.

I didn't tell anyone right away that I had met Jesus and that He was busy working on my soiled heart. I just smiled and listened, and if the opening came into the conversation, I mentioned my new Friend. After that I was hooked. I couldn't go back to my old ways. It was so refreshing to talk to men and have them listen to me. They started to value my input, and it felt good. In fact, it felt better than compliments on my physical features, especially since no matter how beautiful you are, there is always going to be another girl just as beautiful.

I don't mean to spend so much time on something that may not be your issue. You may already respect yourself deeply and wouldn't be caught dead doing some of the things that I was foolish enough to do, but I want to make sure those of you who are like me get the message loud and clear that God has a dream for you, but you have to respect yourself. He has a mission that can only be accomplished from the tender and loving hands of a mother, a sister, a daughter, a girlfriend. I just don't want you to discredit those aspirations through a lack of respect.

I went on a double date with a friend of mine once. We were bowling, and her boyfriend came over to my date and I and casually said something about his sexual relationship with her. My face was instantly heated, and I wanted to drop my big bowling ball on his foot and tell my boyfriend we were leaving. Instead, I gave him a look that showed I was not impressed and made a mental note to discuss it with my friend. When I did finally mention to her what he had said, she didn't seem to care. I tried to explain to her that any guy who would make jokes about their sexual relationship with two people he had just met was not a guy worth her time. He didn't respect her, because if he truly respected her in the first place he would have never been sexually involved or made their relationship the butt of a joke.

I was so hurt by the fact that it didn't seem to bother her one bit. She is an absolutely beautiful girl. She has one of those utterly perfect bodies, and her hair is always thick and silky and beautiful. I wanted her to see what she's really worth. I wanted her to know that she could do so much better, that she deserved someone who respected her and her body, not a guy who used her as a trophy he could brag about to his friends. I tell you these instances because I want you to learn from them. I sincerely wish someone had grabbed me by the hair and told me that I deserved the world and asked me why I was willing to settle.

Although I will be talking about cheating and abstaining from sex until you're married in later chapters, please be aware that both those things fall under the umbrella of respect. A guy who respects you will never pressure you to sleep with him or choose the arms of another girl. Wait for the guy who considers you his queen.

Another way to tell if a guy respects you is how he allows his friends to speak about you. I realize that you may be a great person, but not everyone is going to like you, sometimes not even your boyfriend's best friends. You see, some single guys are threatened when their good friend gets a girlfriend, no matter how great she is. They know that their relationship with him is going to change, so they talk about you behind your back and make harsh comments to your face. If this happens, watch your boyfriend's reaction. If he truly respects you, he will silence them quickly, and they will learn that the two of you are a package deal. If, however, he ignores their comments and tells you to not take his friends seriously, break it off. No guy should ask you to tolerate disrespect from, of all people, his friends. Either he puts them in check or he is basically telling you exactly what you are worth to him, and it clearly is not very much.

Respect. This word and its meaning have somehow been lost in these final days before God comes to take us home. Please remember them in your search for your soul mate. You are a beautiful person, created in God's image. You are worth so much. Don't ever let a guy treat you like an object. There is so much more to you than what is on the outside. Don't get sucked in to the notion that you have to be sexual with a guy for him to like you. If he respects you as a person, he will respect your body and your desire to save yourself for marriage. This is a non-negotiable topic.

Of course, like I said in the beginning, it goes both ways. You can't be hitting on his friends, dressing provocatively, and posting pictures of yourself online that would be better off in a Victoria's Secret catalog and expect him to naturally respect you. Respect is earned. My best advice is to try and live each day as if God was standing beside you—which by the way, He is. You only have one reputation; don't ruin it by flaunting your body and degrading yourself so that men will notice you. You are worth being respected. Please do not sell yourself short.

If You Think He's
The One, Take It Slow

Taking it slow is an art that will only make your future relationship run more smoothly. This is important for several reasons. First of all, as I said before, relationships work best when they are actually rooted in friendship. There is nothing wrong with making sure that the two of you are best friends before getting romantic. Second, if you meet a guy and get the feeling this is what you've been waiting for, let him figure it out for himself. Nothing scares a guy more then an overly pushy woman cramming commitment down his throat when he isn't ready.

If God told you he's the one, He will be sure to help this guy know it too. In the beginning I think it is good to keep a certain level of mystery to your relationship. Don't tell him everything you're thinking or how taken you are with him. You should let him know you are interested, but make sure you don't go overboard. Men are easily scared off. I learned this firsthand. I'll define some of the things I learned a little more clearly later, but to be brief, don't act like he is the first guy to ever approach you. Don't call or text him obsessively. Don't tell his friends you are so in love, and don't tell him he's everything you've been looking for. If you're right, you will have plenty of time to tell him later, but for now, take things slow.

When an ex of mine and I first started seeing each other, I was sure that he was the one. I remember sitting with my mother at our dining room table and beaming with excitement while telling her about my soul mate. He was the one I spoke about earlier who I invited to Thanksgiving dinner with my family near the beginning of our relationship. Of course, that holiday was the beginning and end of my perfect relationship. As he drove me to my grandparents' house, he told me he realized that after spending the day with my family he wasn't ready to be in a serious relationship. He promised me it had nothing to

HLAS-3

do with us, that it just scared him to see himself already so committed before he even asked me to officially be his girlfriend. I held back my tears and pretended I didn't care, but when he dropped me off, I left my heart in the backseat of his car.

I felt incredibly stupid as I faced my family. I had pushed things to move quickly, and regretfully, I knew I had pushed him away. My point is that you can really damage a potentially great relationship simply by not being patient. I am a little bit old-fashioned and believe in letting the man take the lead, but every now and then I take things into my own hands and try to move the relationship along at the speed I want it to go. Over and over again, I have had to learn that the best thing you can do for yourself is to let him pursue you. If he doesn't want to put the effort into trying to woo you than he is not worth it. Girls are prizes to be won. I know it may be hard to bite your tongue, but if you're right and he is the one, in due time you will be able to tell him everything you think and feel for him.

Please don't settle on love. As I have said before, true love must first be found in Christ. All you have to do is ask and God will gladly guide you. But you have to be willing to step back and let Him take control.

As you begin your relationship, you will go on numerous dates and spend time talking to him on the phone or texting him. To help you in the dating process, I have outlined four things I think you should take notice of after your date:

1. Did he listen to you and ask questions about you? Simply put, did he show a genuine interest in getting to know who you are?

2. Did you do the same? Did you ask important questions of him? Based on his responses thus far, is he what you want? Remember, don't get sucked into the esteem-boosting game of trying to snag a guy just so you can say you have a boyfriend and feel better about yourself. Dating is just as much about you finding him as it is about him finding you. Pick wisely.

3. Before you make anything official, hang out with him everywhere! Hang out with him around his family, around your family, around mutual friends, and alone. Make sure you really get to know who he is, and make sure you like what you see in all those settings.

4. Do not call him. If you just met or have only gone on one date, put the phone down. If he is interested, he will call you. Some may consider it old-fashioned, but the truth is that most men are

wired with a desire to chase after the prize. Do not take that away from him. You need to let him initiate all first meetings. After some time, feel free to begin calling and inviting him places, but in the beginning, at least the first three to four dates, make sure he wants you there bad enough to invite you.

Sometimes we are the problem. We chase guys away and don't even know it. We make ourselves too available, or we do the chasing ourselves, and it usually doesn't work. Even if you get him, there will always be this uneven relational pull because you were the pursuer. You will constantly be pursuing him to keep him there and happy. It's not supposed to be like that. Whether he does it through his friends, the Internet, or a simple note, he will usually find a way to get to know you. So sit back and wait for him to come to you.

Friendship is the component so many relationships are missing. Instead, raging hormones take control, and many girls give themselves away in an effort to "hang on" to the man of their dreams. The problem with this plan is that you are giving him the icing before he learns to enjoy the cake. The first step of your relationship needs to be based on a solid friendship. Can you have fun when there's nothing to do? Can you talk on the phone for hours without awkward silence? Make sure the two of you enjoy each other's company and not just each other's looks.

As friends you should be able to talk about anything and everything. Healthy communication is a big part of any successful relationship. If the two of you are constantly sharing your thoughts and feelings, you are going to naturally move forward in your relationship. After you've been dating for a while, you may feel like you know everything there is to know about one another, but don't stop asking questions and talking to each other. If that happens, your relationship is doomed. As humans we crave the acceptance of others. If you are not listening to him and asking for his opinion, he may seek that kind of support from someone else. In my experience I've learned that in order to make a relationship work you have to keep doing things together. Activities keep a familiar relationship fresh. Try something new together—go to the arcade and play games, host a game night with friends, go to dinner, see a movie, go fishing! All these different things will keep the two of you talking and falling in love all over again.

I recognize that it's hard to take things slow when your stomach has butterflies and you melt in his presence, but you need to build your relationship on the solid foundation of friendship so that it can stand the test of time. If he's the one, you are going to have the rest of your life to let the romantic sparks fly.

On the other hand, I want you to be aware of when it's too slow. Some guys say that they want to take it slow so that they can keep looking to make sure there is nothing better out there. If you've been in the same position for almost a year or more, maybe you should move on. Give him an ultimatum. Either he wants to progress or he doesn't. Just make sure you are prepared to do what's best for you. If he's holding on to you in case no one better comes along, you need to open your eyes and set sail.

For some guys commitment is a really hard thing to swallow. He may like you a lot, but not enough to shut down all his other options. But think about this, if you were everything he ever wanted, he would do everything within his power to keep you. Don't make excuses for yourself and for him. He may like you, but it may not be enough, and that's OK! You will find someone who likes you more than enough!

Just remember that in the beginning, although it goes against your bubbling emotions, you need to sit back and let him pursue you. Take things slow, and let them progress when you both are ready. But most importantly, pray! Let God know how you are feeling and ask Him to lead you in the right direction.

Cheating . . .
Pretty Much a Deal Breaker

You wouldn't want a cheater on your team, so you shouldn't want one in your future either. If he cheats at the beginning part of your relationship while you're dating, he is not ready to make a commitment.

The key to remember in dealing with a cheating boyfriend is that he chose someone over you. Break it off, and let him have her. I think it's pretty vital that you really digest that statement. If he is pleading with you for forgiveness, you really need to let that thought resonate in your head—he actually already chose someone else over you. There is really no decision on your part to be made. He didn't give you the dignity or respect to decide whether or not you wanted to continue the relationship. He chose for you, and it's over.

Now this is not to say that people cannot change. I am a firm believer that God can mend the heart of anyone who places themselves in His hands. With time, maturity, and help from God, the two of you may find each other again. My point is that I would not drop everything and wait for him to prove to you he is sorry. Move on with your life, date other people, and then see what happens. The truth is that once trust is breached the odds of things working out are extremely slim. You will always be questioning where he is and who he is with; you will constantly want to search his phone or computer; you will always be on edge and for good reason. It will not be possible for you to be truly happy without being able to trust him. You'll always be wondering, "OK, when is he going to slip up again." And every girl in his life will become your possible enemy. The best way to see if there could be a possible future for the two of you is to move on and see how you feel toward him after analyzing things from a clear and non-biased perspective. Get away from him and let your head clear.

If he cheated before you were officially dating, I think that shows you he is not yet ready for commitment. That may change, but it may not. You need to make sure that he is the kind of person you want to sit around and wait for. Of course, if you were not officially dating, I'm not sure if it qualifies as cheating. In this instance, I recommend evaluating the differences between where you are in your desires and where he is.

A big mistake I think women often make when they are confronted with the issue of cheating is to blame the other woman. She is not the one who promised she loved you; she is not the one who held you while you cried; she is not the one you thought you could always count on. This has nothing to do with her, because she has nothing to do with you. For all you know she could be a victim just like you. If you focus your anger on the "other" woman, you are making a big mistake and playing yourself right into his hands. Your boyfriend would love for her to be the villain because then the two of you can focus on her as the problem and you will never address what he has done. This is not about her. This is about what he did to you. He broke his promises. You entrusted him with your heart, and he was careless. Direct all your animosity and anger where it belongs—on the cheater.

Of course, this cheating thing goes both ways. If you are serious about someone, he deserves all your attention. Don't answer phone calls from your ex-boyfriends or be flirtatious with other guy friends. I've noticed that girls often try to make their boyfriends jealous to assure themselves that the guys are into them. That's immature. I used to be guilty of this until one day my father sat me down and reminded me of the importance of not being that petty.

You see, guys are naturally territorial. They are wired with certain desires to take care of and protect the object of their affection. The dumbest thing you can do is to play off those desires by trying to start a fight for him. You should shut down all confrontation by making clear where you stand. If a guy hits on you while you are out with your boyfriend, shut him down. Don't play it up in order to create drama. Don't go running to him and tell him that there is some guy in class who may be interested in you. It is your job, not his, to show these guys you are taken. If you want to be a good girlfriend, you have to stop playing games. You have to do things with his best interest in mind.

Cheating is extremely hurtful. It's literally spitting in the face of your significant other, and I don't think it is Christ-like or lady-like to do that to anyone. If you like someone else, break up with him. And the same goes for the guy. Wouldn't you rather have him break up with you than sneak around behind your back with another woman? This book is not about dating, it's about finding your husband, and if that is what you are really trying to do, you are going to have to change the way you have done things in the past. You shouldn't stay with someone who cheats on you because you're scared that you won't find someone else. Don't fall into that evil trap.

I really want to drive home the idea that if he cheated on you it needs to be over. Girls, especially nowadays, are becoming more and more inclined to make excuses for their boyfriends. We feel so dependent on them that we want to blot out and forget anything they did that would warrant a breakup. You can't imagine life without him, so you excuse any behavior as long as he stays with you. That's not logical thinking, especially if you are looking for a soul mate. If you are actually looking for your life partner, that method is inexcusable and is no way to live. We're talking about the rest of your life! I think that is something I wasn't always realistic about in my past. Don't let the person you are with distract you emotionally or mentally from putting your best foot forward in this life—which is the only life you have. If worrying about him takes up all your energy, that's a problem.

The best thing I ever realized is that you have to live life in the here and now. You cannot look at the potential you see in him and wish and hope for the day when he fulfills that. You have to look at who he is right now, in the present, and decide if that is someone you want to be with forever—and be honest with yourself.

I think trust is the lifeline of a relationship. As long as the two of you can trust each other, you can probably get through anything. However, once trust is gone everything will begin to collapse and burn. If he has cheated and broken your trust, you need to let him go. No matter how hard it seems, you need to move on. Like I said before, he already made the choice for you. He put his immediate wants before your feelings. Even if he tells you he was not thinking clearly, he put himself in the position to make that decision. He will probably try to blame his actions on a variety of things, but in the end, it was his choice to make. No one was holding a gun to his head.

This whole cheating escapade is something I feel really passionate about because I have watched people close to me become completely destroyed as a result of cheating. I have seen gorgeous women be reduced to crazy, raging control freaks all because he cheated and she stayed. Love is not supposed to be painful. It is not supposed to rip your heart into pieces, and it is not supposed to hurt. It is supposed to build you up and bring you joy. You deserve so much better than to be someone else's afterthought. If you aren't on the forefront of his brain all the time, he probably isn't the one for you.

Another reason I am unsympathetic to cheaters is because I know guys. They have been my major form of friendship for years. I have been in the trenches, ladies, and heard with my own ears the uncensored version of these cheating conversations, and I was honestly repelled to hear friend after friend laugh about how he cheated on his girlfriend. Sure, if they were ever caught, they would pull out all the stops, let the waterworks run, and beg for forgiveness, but I'll never forget hearing those guys callously talk about their girlfriends like they meant nothing.

The truth is that everything isn't always as it seems, and some guys can't be trusted. Fortunately, there are good guys out there, but make sure you let go of the bad ones until you find the right one for you. I have certainly had guy friends who were inspirational people and who could be taken at their word. But there are enough worms in enough apples that should cause you to take caution before "biting" into a relationship.

I personally have never been cheated on, or if I have, they did a good job at keeping it a secret because I never found out. It's not because I am so great that no guy would want to risk losing me, it's simply because I've never been attracted to the kind of guy who seemed like a cheater. If I was seeing a guy who showed me any signs of possible future cheating, I was out of there. That simply was not ever attractive to me.

The good thing is that if you are following my advice from the previous chapters you are minimizing the risk of dating a cheater. Guys who sincerely respect you and show you they respect you by doing the things we talked about earlier usually aren't cheaters. If you take the time to get to know the person you are with before dating, odds are their true colors will shine through before things get too serious. I realize that some girls are attracted to the bad boy. They want to tame the guy that no other girl can because it will make them feel beautiful. Believe me, you are hanging on to a slippery rope. Seek out the guys with impeccable characters, the ones who respect women and God.

Relationships, I suppose, will always be a gamble, but don't be blind to the things that will better your odds.

Some things to look for in the personality of someone who may be a cheater are things like selfishness and a need for instant gratification. If he has been caught lying before, is often unavailable, is insensitive toward other people's feelings, flirts with your friends in front of your face, is inconsistent, or is secretive, be cautious and let the warning signs speak for themselves. I think the absolute best way to tell if you are with a possible cheater is to simply trust your gut. God gave us a pretty good intuition for a reason, and you are not helping yourself at all by not using it.

The other problem with cheating is that it's usually habitual. Once a person realizes that they can get away with something like that, they tend to do it again. Also, people don't change overnight. If he had a girlfriend when you met him but was coming on to you, odds are you will be his next victim. If you are serious about looking for your husband, you need to treat all acts of dishonesty as such. This is not just a boyfriend you are dealing with, so the problem really is much greater than if you treated it that way. This is your potential husband, and the odds are just too great to risk a disastrous marriage, especially with huge warning signs while you're dating.

The reason I'm spending so much time on this topic is because it is becoming an American epidemic. Statistics show that an estimated 22 percent of men cheat and more than 50 percent of marriages end in divorce. The odds are not in our favor, girls, and the truth is it isn't always easy to spot them. Cheaters usually are extremely charming, seem sincere, and shower you with attention. As I've said before, if a guy is quick to tell you he loves you, that he can see himself marrying you, or anything else that would usually take a lot of thought before blurting out, the odds are that he has dished out those very same lines before. People don't put themselves there quickly unless they have nothing to lose.

Don't beat yourself up if you've been a victim and didn't spot it, because sometimes it is hard to see what we don't want to. It's important for you to be aware of the problems though while you are seeking your mate. You don't just want to be married. You want to be married to the man of your dreams. You want to be with the man whom God created with you in mind; you want the father of your children and your future lover to be honest and dependable. Like I said before, relationships are hard even when everything is going perfectly. It is not going to help your cause if you are shooting yourself in the foot by not being cautious with whom you pick.

As a woman, you also need to recognize what you may be doing that could signal these types of guys your way. If you are looking for your soul mate at parties, dressed provocatively, or by trying to steal him from someone else, you are making yourself a target. Great guys don't approach you because you're showing a lot of skin. They don't look for wives in miniskirts who look like they could be on a street corner. Great guys usually find great women who are intelligent and strong. Remember, people can't walk all over you unless you lie down first. If you portray yourself as a tramp, he is probably going to treat you like one. If you want to be taken seriously, you have to first learn what it means to hold yourself like a lady and how to love yourself for who you are. Once you love and respect yourself, people will see that, and you will start attracting men who know you are a serious woman.

As I said at the beginning of this chapter, if you discover that you're with a cheater, get out of the relationship. However, I do realize that it's easier said than done to say goodbye, especially if you have been together for a long time. You have history and fond memories, and you just don't know if you can live without him. But trust me, you can. It will hurt a lot, and it may take you months or years to get over him, but you have to try. Your future is at stake. Just think about how much more it would hurt if you walked down the aisle, had a baby together, and then found out he was cheating again.

It's going to hurt, but it's for the best. If you are genuinely trying to get over an ex, get rid of all the things that remind you of him, including pictures, letters, and gifts. Sitting in your room snuggling up to his T-shirt isn't going to help you move on—it is going to make you relive the good memories over and over.

If you are angry and depressed, that's OK. You lost a piece of yourself during this relationship, and I think it is healthy to let yourself go through these emotions. The death of a relationship can feel like a death altogether. You have a right to mourn, and you shouldn't listen to friends who command you to bounce right back. Take your time and do things when you are ready. Depending on how deep your relationship was, you may need to see a counselor, or if you have a couple of good friends who don't mind hearing the same story over and over for your sake, you can talk things through with them.

It is good for you to be around friends and family who love you and remind you that you deserve better than this. Read books, watch movies, start a new hobby, work out, and take care of yourself. The better you look, the better you are going to feel. Do things that get your mind to focus on something other than the breakup.

The most important part of the moving-on process is to date again. Don't let him ruin you for life. There are terrible people out there, but you are now all the wiser to spotting them. Wait till you are ready, and then get out there and meet someone new. The worst thing you can do is to let him set the bar for your self-esteem. The problem was with him, not you. If he didn't see you for the gem you are, it just means the two of you were not a perfect fit. It does not mean that you were not pretty enough or smart enough or loveable enough. Now your options are open; the ball is in your court. Get out there and snag your soul mate.

Let's Talk About Sex

Sex. It is the inevitable topic every couple has to talk about at some point. Should you do it before marriage, or should you wait? A friend of mine once said, regarding sex, "I wouldn't buy a pair of shoes without trying them on first." Unfortunately, that is the pervading thought process of our society. But regardless of how society treats sex and love, your future husband is not a pair of shoes. Although this sounds so cliché, true love can wait. The best gift a bride can give her husband on their wedding night is her virginity. Waiting until you're married to have sex is really a sign of faith—a faith in God that He would bring you your soul mate.

My parents talked to me about sex, but all they ever really said was not to do it before marriage. Looking back I wish someone would have sat me down and said what I am about to say to you: sex is really only great when you love the person you're experiencing it with and know that you will be together for the rest of your lives. True love can't be rushed, and it isn't fleeting. True love, in my opinion, will usually only come once in your life. If you hear your friends talking about who they hooked up with last weekend and how incredible it was, they are lying. Either they are lying or they have no idea how much more it could have been if they were with their forever partner, so much so that they can't even fathom it.

Here's the thing that most people don't ever think about. We, as a human race, didn't create sex. Since we didn't create it, we have no idea how to use it correctly or how it really works. Sex is not a sin. God created it for us, but He created it to be experienced within the confines of marriage. It is the deepest form of couple worship, thanking Him for the gift of each other. Sex was created to be enjoyed. Being the creative, thoughtful, and gentle Lord that He is, God created us to be sexual beings, knowing that it would fulfill us. Adam and Eve were the first married couple to consummate their marriage in the most intimate way possible—they are our example of what God planned when He created sex.

As I grew older, I became a firm believer in the thought process that virginity is the best gift a husband and wife can give each other on their wedding night. Not only does it put the words "I love you" into physical form, but it expresses how much you loved each other before you even knew each other! By waiting, you are saying to your future soul mate, "I knew that one day I would find you, and so I saved myself for this moment. I wanted to share this precious gift with no one else but you." Sex is meant to be a connection between the two of you that makes you one person.

Unfortunately, with so many things in life, Satan has perverted and demeaned sex, making it a common practice instead of the sacred act that it is. You see, the whole Christian experience is about dying to self and only living for the sole purpose of that which Christ has created you to fulfill. Sex outside of marriage, drugs, alcohol, and other temptations are all about self-gratification. It's all about living life on your rules and terms, finding happiness apart from God. The Bible talks repeatedly about sexual immorality. It is a perversion that will separate you from God. Satan is no fool; he knows if he can get you hooked on the idea of self-gratification you and God will no longer have anything in common. God is all about true love, the type that allowed him to hang on the cross for the sake of your salvation.

Self-gratification is something that is not in God's genetic makeup. When you start to indulge in these things, your appetite will never be satisfied. You will slip further and further away from Him because you're playing with an action that wasn't meant to be used under those terms. It wasn't meant to be casual. It's our deeply perverted society that has made us believe it doesn't really mean anything. Christ and the apostles were very intent on the message of sexual purity.

In Acts when the disciples met together to discuss the important tenets of the early Christian church, which included Jews and Gentiles, sex was at the top of their list. The disciples met together, prayed, and came up with a list of teachings that they felt God had given them. Teaching people the importance of sexual purity was on that list. They knew that Christians were called to be set apart and that dabbling in the self-gratifications of sex outside of marriage would not be acceptable to Christ.

Now, I believe strongly in sexual purity because I believe deeply in God. But I think the case can be made whether you are seeking to live a life acceptable to Christ's standards or not. The reason is because you are special. You are beautiful. You have something worth preserving. Your body is one of a kind, and you shouldn't pass it around to random people who aren't going to appreciate it for the classic piece of art that it is. Sure, your boyfriend may tell you he loves you, and that may satisfy you enough to allow him to experience everything you have to offer, but the true symbol of love that has withstood even our morally-lost society is marriage. Marriage is a big deal. It is the testament between two people that says you are committed to love one another until the day you depart from this earth. It says that God has entrusted you to care for this person and that with this person you will actually create tiny people.

Marriage, when done earnestly, is love in action. Sex, which is only meant after marriage, is a by-product of that love. Regardless of what you've heard from anyone else, sex is personal, it is special, and you are making a huge mistake if you give it to someone who isn't your spouse. I can promise you that you will regret it if you have sex before marriage when you meet the one person you would die to give everything to. When you meet him, everything you've read that you thought may be fluff will become so real to you. It will actually cut your soul that you stole that piece of beauty that was meant for him and gave it to someone else so much less deserving. Someone else who probably used you or left you or who ended up breaking your heart to pieces because that love wasn't real. It was a counterfeit that you tried to pass off as authentic, and only when you meet that one person who can pick up all those broken pieces and put them back together will you probably ever truly grasp the severity of what you've done.

The thing about sex is that I'm going to assume that most people have made some type of sexually impure mistake outside of marriage, including me. If you have made a mistake, don't get trapped in the thought process that you are beyond repair, so why even try. You can be "pure" again through repentance and a change of heart. The Bible is pretty clear that once God forgives you He tosses your blemish like a stone far from His mind and recognizes with great pride the change that you've made. Jesus actually told His disciples that nothing gives Him greater joy than the child that comes home from the deepest of pits. These hearts, He says, become even more precious than those who have never strayed, and there is celebration in heaven because someone who was lost has come home. I've felt His joy and peace when I myself came home after being completely lost. In fact, there were times I made a conscious effort to turn away from the direction He was guiding me and forge my own path. He waited patiently and never gave up on me until I came back, and when I did, without hesitation He made me new.

Even now, sometimes I feel as though God is far from me. Like He's turned His back to me because He's frustrated with the continual mistakes I make. We, as humans, can only tell someone not to do something so many times before we get angry if they don't listen. And to be honest, sometimes I feel like God is angry with me.

Sometimes I avoid prayer, hoping that what I have done will blow over in His mind and He will forget. And when I do pray, it's about surface things. I refrain from asking Him anything that would require me to dig deeper and ask something of myself. I'll put our relationship on stand-by because I can't bear to call His name, knowing I've made a fool of Him before the heavenly hosts.

The thought that usually puts me into such deep sorrow that I can't sleep at night is the thought that I sinned on purpose. It wasn't an accident; it was a choice, a choice I made, again. I have a hard time sleeping at night when I think of the way I betrayed Him. I quit trying to avoid sin because of fear a long time ago. I used to try hard to make perfect decisions because I was scared of His wrath. I realized, however, that God isn't supposed to be served out of fear but out of love, and that's how I try to treat Him now.

Now, when I choose Satan's lies over God's wisdom (and that is what I'm doing when I sin), I feel wrecked with grief, not out of fear but out of the sheer pain I know God must feel when I choose the enemy over His friendship. Only in dealing with God and Satan would we ever do that. No one in their right mind would ever have any sort of dealings with the complete enemy of someone they loved in any other circumstance than spiritual matters. It just wouldn't happen. Loyalty is a value in American society. It's a virtue that is sought. We can forgive a lot of other digressions in one another, as long as we feel loyalty.

God must often be lonely. Thousands, even millions, claim to be His friend yet they neglect that one defining piece of a true friendship; pure and utter loyalty. That should be your common denominator between purity and Christ. We should avoid sin on that basis alone. Not because we fear the consequences, not because we want to feel good about ourselves, not because we want to be respected as a spiritual beacon—I'd even go as far as to say not because we want to go to heaven—but we should avoid sin on the purely sincere basis of our complete submission through love and loyalty to God. We should turn our backs to Satan's temptations because the thought of coordinating any type of trade with the enemy of our Father is vile to us.

And so when I do mess up, when I do exhibit how weak my friendship is, when I'm a traitor to the Best Friend I've ever had, I sometimes feel as though He wants nothing to do with me, and that thought hurts. However, I read a thought once in *Steps To Christ*, a precious book written by Ellen White, that comforted me.

She wrote, ". . . the enemy of good blinded the minds of men, so that they looked upon God with fear; they thought of Him as severe and unforgiving. Satan led men to conceive of God as a being whose chief attribute is stern justice, one who is a severe judge, a harsh, exacting creditor."

As I read those words, I was humbled. I realized that God, the same God who I had been avoiding and who I had written off through my surface-level prayers, was speaking to me. He made an effort to seek me out, and in His ever-powerful mercy, God reminded me that His mission to earth was not to tally the errors of men, but to scribble them in the sand. I had forgotten that God is love, and Ellen White reminded me that not only is God love but that I need to reciprocate that love through loyalty. So please, remember, God is not the creator of guilt, Satan is. Satan wants you to believe that God is angry. He wants you to avoid Him and bury your casket so deep into the ground that you don't even know how to get back home. Satan wants you to believe that God is tired of forgiving you, but I hope you know that Jesus is love.

You see, that's part of Satan's deception. He banks on the fact that we will assess ourselves and come up short. He hopes that we'll find ourselves dirty in God's eyes and thus give up and come to his camp completely. Guilt is not an emotion God created. God gave us a conscience, but He is also all about free will. If we choose to ignore that still, small voice, He is not going to soak us in guilt because that was our choice. Satan is the orchestrator of guilt. He knows that guilt becomes repressive, and too much repression will cause depression. If he can sell us on the valid point that we are not good enough for God, we will give up.

It works because it's true. We aren't fit for the company of Christ, but nevertheless, He promises that through His mercy if we call on Him He'll be there. There is literally no sin—from sex to murder—that God won't forgive when we are truly sorry. I'm not just saying this; it's in the Bible. If you want to meet a bunch of sinners unworthy of Christ's love, flip through the pages in God's Holy Word. The stories of King David, Moses, Jonah, Adam and Eve, and countless others show us that it is possible to change. God knows more than anyone how hard this life is because He lived it. He made Himself forever God and forever man so that He could walk in our footsteps. The devil doesn't want you to know that our God is a God of forgiveness. He's hoping that we won't figure out the fact that our Father gives us so much grace we could never even begin to reap the benefits from every tear He's wiped from our eyes.

Don't let Satan win this battle. Don't let him score any points in the match between good and evil. Saving sex for marriage isn't just about a commitment to your earthly mate, it's a commitment between you and your heavenly Father. It's also about a commitment between you and yourself. No matter what mistakes you've made in the past, let God take those mistakes today and cast them away. It's time to make a clean start.

If this comes across as being pushy, I'm sorry. I just really want to share with you what I wish someone had sat down and taken the time to truly dive into with me. The fact is that it is hard to be a girl. Guys are constantly trying to get physical with you, and it's tiring to keep your guard up. But you have to be strong and hold firm to your beliefs. You have to ignore the boys and a culture that tells you that sex is no big deal.

This chapter is not about making you feel bad about yourself if you've made a mistake. You may have trusted too quickly or thought you were in love or been seeking reassurance. No matter what the reason, God knows all about it. He knows your heart better than you do, and He still looks at you with the most loving eyes. God knows where your life was then, and He knows where you are now. God can make your body pure again if you will ask Him to.

But what about if you are going to get married, is it OK to have sex with your boyfriend if you are planning on getting married? Unfortunately, you may think you are going to get married, but until you walk down the aisle and say "I do," things can change. I can honestly say that with all three of my extremely serious boyfriends I thought I would marry them. I spent about three years of my life with each of them, and at the time, I was positive things would end up with a white picket fence. Thank God for unanswered prayers. He never made it 100 percent clear that I had found the one, so although I wanted desperately to settle down and stop the dating game, I chose not to settle for someone who wasn't a part of God's plans.

Not only is sex outside of marriage bad for your future mate but it is also bad for you. A woman's primary sex organ is her heart. When you see girls out there sleeping with a different guy every weekend, don't sit and talk bad about them. They're hurting, and they're trying to fill a void in their heart that they think sex will fill, but it doesn't work. Although sex before marriage may not be something you struggle with, it may be for some of your friends. If this is the case, be a good example, and tell your friend that she is better than that. Remind her that she deserves so much more than to be some guy's conquest.

God can use you to touch someone else's life. You have a duty to share the things that God has placed on your heart in a loving way. The Bible says that God will hold us accountable for the way we have impacted someone else's life. It's all about love—you have to do for others what no one did for you. You have to go out on a limb and love the unlovable. Don't be the typical mean gossip girl. Love her, love yourself.

I had a friend once ask me where in the Bible it explicitly says that premarital sex is wrong. She knew it was, but her boyfriend, who was also a Christian, had told her that the Bible doesn't actually say that. I gave her a few verses that are highlighted in my Bible, and I want to share them with you also, and hopefully you can share them with someone else. I would also like you to sign the purity contract at the end of this book, and then rip it out and put it where you know you will glance at it from time to time.

Feel free to write some of these verses on your purity contract or highlight them in your Bible, but above all, let God convict you of His truths for your life. (These verses were taken from the New International Version.)

- 1 Corinthians 6:9 says, "Do you not know that the wicked will not inherit the kingdom of God? Do not be deceived: Neither the sexually immoral nor idolaters nor adulterers nor male prostitutes nor homosexual offenders . . ."

- 1 Corinthians 6:13 says, " 'Food for the stomach and the stomach for food'—but God will destroy them both. The body is not meant for sexual immorality, but for the Lord, and the Lord for the body."
- 2 Timothy 2:22 deals more with the importance of purity of heart altogether: "Flee the evil desires of youth, and pursue righteousness, faith, love and peace, along with those who call on the Lord out of a pure heart."
- 1 Corinthians 6:18 says, "Flee from sexual immorality. All other sins a man commits are outside his body, but he who sins sexually sins against his own body."
- Ephesians 5:3 says, "But among you there must not be even a hint of sexual immorality, or of any kind of impurity, or of greed, because these are improper for God's holy people."
- Colossians 3:5 says, "Put to death, therefore, whatever belongs to your earthly nature: sexual immorality, impurity, lust, evil desires and greed, which is idolatry."
- And here is the one that speaks the strongest to me because of the Bible's references to the acts of Sodom and Gomorrah and the final days of Noah as a predictor of what the end of time will be like before God returns. Jude 1:7 says, "In a similar way, Sodom and Gomorrah and the surrounding towns gave themselves up to sexual immorality and perversion. They serve as an example of those who suffer the punishment of eternal fire."

These are just a few verses I have selected, but if you read your Bible, sexual immorality is obviously a problem the Lord knew we would face because it is spoken against countless times.

The Calm Before the Storm

This, at least for me, is probably the hardest part of this whole thing. This is the stage right before lightning strikes, and that means that you have to be single and sometimes for quite awhile. Sometimes it takes being single and observing others to be more aware of what you want and need in another person. I know that this stage sucks. It sucks a lot. No one wants to be alone. But remember this, when all is calm, when you least expect it, that's when it strikes. That is when everything else will all make sense. Don't jump into a relationship with a guy you're just keeping around for comfort, and cut it off with your ex-boyfriend for good. This is just you time. You have to be patient during this time. Figure out what makes you tick, and what you think God wants you to accomplish with your life. You are about to build a team, remember? So you need to make sure you can pull your weight.

For a long time I can remember asking God why He wasn't acting on my behalf. I was sure I was ready, and I wanted Him to bless me with my soul mate. I had this Bible teacher my freshmen year of college who first opened my eyes to the importance of finding the right mate. He said that God cared about that kind of stuff. Love was, after all, His specialty. My teacher quickly captured the attention of the entire lecture hall as he spoke to a room full of young adults all sure that here, in college, was where they'd find their soul mate. The girls especially were practically hanging on his every word, and then he challenged us to pray about it. He said to pray for God to have an angel bring you His pick for you if you were ready for it.

I was already pretty confident I was with the right person, but as soon as things with him went down in flames, I dropped to my knees and started to pray. I met other guys, but I knew they weren't the right ones. I continued praying this prayer, but looking back on it, I realize that I hindered my prayer because I got back together with my ex-boyfriend. That act showed a lack of faith on my part and that was a direct hindrance to God. I often think that because of my inability to enjoy the calm before the storm, I've ruined it. I wish my Bible teacher would've made that part clear when he had that room of freshmen girls squeezing their eyes tight, praying for God to have an angel bring them their soul mates. One girl in that class who probably prayed the prayer got married before the school year even ended. She and her husband now have a baby. The two of them weren't even dating the day my teacher gave us the challenge. I don't even know if they were friends. She was ready though, and so when she prayed, with no hindrances to her words, God acted on her behalf. She was ready, but apparently I wasn't.

Sometimes as women we think we are so certain of what we want. We think we've got it all together and aren't sure what the hold up is on God's end. Just remember, it is possible that the wait is on the guy's end. It could be that he is not ready, and if you met now things just wouldn't work out. It could be that, or it could be you. I'm not saying you have to be perfect before God will answer this prayer, but I think it will definitely help if you are the best person you can be. Think about this stage as your cocoon stage. This is your time to sit and piece things together. Get right with God, and figure out the things about yourself that are great and the things that may need some prayer and changing. My point here is that we are quick to think there is nothing wrong with us, and we don't understand why we aren't getting what we want, but sometimes the problem is us.

This isn't just about how some guy is going to come into your life and everything will work. You have to learn how to make things work when it is just you. He deserves to meet you at your best. You deserve to be at your best for your own self-esteem, let alone another person. If you want to lose a few pounds, this is the time to do it. If you want to finish your education, go to school. If you want to travel and see the world, book the tickets. Things are going to be wonderful when he is added to the picture, but it will also become more complicated. You can ease some of those future complications by making sure that even alone, you are happy. You cannot look to someone else to fix you. It isn't fair to put that kind of pressure on him. He is not a knight on a white horse who is going to save you from who you are right now. He is the cherry. He's the over-the top kind of blessing you never thought could have existed. He's dessert after an already amazing meal. He's everything you think you don't deserve. He's going to be the difference between good and extraordinary. So you need to make sure that all your pieces are aligned.

I was never really good at what I just described. I wasn't happy alone, and that's why all my breakups were dragged on for eons when they should have just been over. I probably hurt really great guys by leading them down a road I knew would come to a dead end. I am ashamed of who I was. They didn't deserve to be treated that callously just because I clearly had some strange emotional issues that scared me from being alone. I'm not sure why I felt I always needed a guy to be interested in me for me to feel interesting. I do know now though that that is not healthy. Believe me when I tell you that you're actually prolonging the entire process by not dealing with your baggage and moving on with your life. Bond with your girlfriends, read books, hang out with your family—the point is to learn how to feel comfortable in your own skin.

I also had this thing when I was single that I had to always like somebody. It's what kept things interesting. This probably isn't a good idea either. This may sound drastic, but until you are comfortable being you, you really need to nix romantic involvement of any kind. It will just hinder your progress and judgment. You'll begin telling yourself you are interested in guys you really aren't just because you're bored. It's time to open the jar, and let all the lightning bugs fly free. This is going to be therapeutic. It is OK to be single. It doesn't mean something is wrong with you; in fact it means you have high standards and aren't settling. When the time is right, lightning will strike.

It reminds me of a hot summer day in July. I was sitting on the sofa in my living room with my body tucked into a ball. I had my face pressed to the window, staring at the gray sky. Each blade of grass stood paralyzed, and everything seemed surreal. It was as if the earth was standing still—everything was completely silent. Then it happened. From the west, I heard a boom and crackling rip of thunder, and I felt my heart begin to speed up. I would have been terrified if I hadn't been witness to this same scene so many times already. Before I knew it, the thunder was roaring and splats of rain came bursting through the clouds. The once serene picture was now a forest of activity. You couldn't even blink your eyes because if you did you would miss the lightning, which was the best part. I had this picture in my head of God standing on a rain cloud somewhere in heaven and throwing these brilliant bursts of light toward earth. They were like spears hurdling toward us, and no matter the distance, I was always able to see them. Sometimes they'd just crackle in the sky and other times they'd seem to strike the ground with the force of God's speed. Lightning to me is beautiful. There is literally nothing else like it.

That's why I centered this book around it, because love really is that same type of concept. They say the odds of getting struck by lightning are the same as winning the million-dollar lottery. Sadly, in this world it seems that true love is just as rare. The problem isn't that it's no longer out there, it's that people feel a little bit of rain and they think it must be it so they grab hands and run inside. They see the sparkle of a firefly, and they don't think it can get better than that. Or perhaps some are even struck with the fiercest of bolts but just don't know how to contain that kind of fire. It's all about love. It's about learning to love people for the gems they truly are. If you think you are the best thing that ever happened to the planet, odds are that that conceit is going to taint any relationship you attempt. Two people who love themselves more than each other will never work. Real love takes self-sacrifice, it takes saying you're sorry, and it takes patience. So be still, take care of yourself, and trust me, when that thunder roars and the rain falls, you'll not only see and hear the rip and crack of the bright lights in the distance, but that lightning will be so close, you'll feel its warmth.

You Know You've Been Struck When . . .

As I conclude this book, I feel as though at this point we have really tackled all the topics that may come up in your dating life. For me, this book was everything I wish my big sister would have written down and handed me before I started high school. Consider yourself my little sister—I hope that you can learn from my mistakes and that everything works out for you. I am more than confident, however, that if you follow God's leading and the common sense advice in this book, you'll be on your way to perfection in no time. Not just with your potential lightning bolt, but as a person.

Just remember that getting the right guy is about you just as much as it is about him. I know girls tend to sit around hoping *he* calls, hoping *he* likes you, and hoping *he* thinks you're pretty, but c'mon, *he* is going to be the lucky one here. You're going to get it all together and be some guy's lifeline. Make sure you are picky. You can afford to be picky. Make sure he sweeps you off your feet and warms your heart like no one else has. This isn't about happy, or good, or fine; this is all about finding that extraordinary connection that probably only comes once in a lifetime. This is about getting struck by lightning—you're never going to be the same.

I would like to touch on a couple key things you can look for when making your list of what you want in someone else. In my opinion the biggest thing to look for in someone else is a guy who genuinely makes you want to be a better person. If he is the one, he is going to become a huge part of who you are. You want to look for someone who makes you want to succeed. Someone who makes you feel beautiful, who makes you laugh, and who reinforces in your mind the reality of God and the importance of living each day in pursuit of a deeper relationship with Him.

Regardless of the confusion that can occur, this life really is all about giving glory to God. You see, Jesus knew it would be hard for us to live alone and accomplish our mission on earth without a human partner, so He made us in pairs. He gave us counterparts whom we can connect with and who can hold us accountable through love. This isn't so we can judge each other and point out all our past mistakes; it is so we can have someone to love us unconditionally as He does. As a couple, you want him to do good because what's good for him is good for you. You want him to succeed because you could brag about how amazing he is all day to anyone who will listen. He wants the same for you because love breeds happiness.

I'm not sure that I can give you any concrete advice as to how you will know whether or not he is the one. Only you can know that. I can tell you that for me, prayer has been essential. Ask God for a definitive answer, and if he's the one, God will show you. But be sure that if you don't feel like God is responding, that that could quite possibly be your answer. You have to constantly pray and read your Bible so that when God speaks you are trained to His voice. I know I talked a lot about God in this book, and it may have caught you off guard to ask God for dating advice, but God is the best Father you are ever going to have. Just like an earthly daddy wants the best for his baby girl, your heavenly Father is even more cautious with your heart. He's got your smile embedded into His memory, and I promise you that He wants you to be happy.

My dad once told me that all a father ever wants is for his daughter to be with a man who loves her as much or more as her dad does. If you are blessed to have an amazing father-daughter relationship, let that guide you. Find the guy who thinks you are just as incredible as your dad has been telling you you are. If you don't have that kind of relationship with your dad, God has allowed us to call him Abba, which means daddy. He will be that father figure for you, and if you ask Him to choose your husband, He will jump at the chance to be included in that aspect of your life.

That's the great thing about God—He is 100 percent in your corner. It's silly not to include Him in this. Sure you can make your own decisions and pick for yourself, but if you want a surefire path to euphoria, Christ is your "go to" dating guru. He cares. Who you spend the rest of your life with will affect who you become, and God is all over that.

Remember to make your list and stick to it! It's easy to throw all common sense out the window when staring into a pair of perfect blue, green, brown, or honey-colored eyes. Rationale is nothing but a thought in the wind when he smiles and calls you baby. You are stronger than this! When you get home from a date, look at your list and see how he matches up. Think about the things that are actually essential to your life and the things you can live without. Look at who he is today and be realistic. Don't try to change him or mother him through some growth period. If you can't take him as he is, you don't need or want him. It will be easier to let him go now rather than months or years from now when you've spent all this time together and your feelings are stronger than your logic.

Keep your ground, and if this guy is nothing but a pretty face, set him free because he is probably someone else's everything. This isn't about finding the guy that all the girls want—it's about finding your guy. This doesn't mean that there is anything wrong with the guy you don't connect with; it just means that there is something missing between the two of you that just won't let things work.

On the flip side, don't be unrealistic. No one is going to be perfect. If you are looking for a perfect guy, you probably fall under the conceited section I talked about in the last chapter. No relationship is going to be perfect. You are going to fight, yell, and possibly lose your temper from time to time. Relationships are a lot of work even when everything is running smoothly. Even the best of relationships are not perfect. It's the love that makes them perfect. It's the love that forces you to want to work it out with this person even though they can drive you crazy. Love is an unstoppable force, and when you find it in its purest form, please hold tight and never let go. Just remember that true love is reciprocated; it doesn't work well one-sided, and even if you haven't met him yet, please do not settle. He will come, and you may not realize it now but God always does everything exactly on time.

The thing I really wanted to focus on in this book is making sure that you are not settling and that you are with someone who just makes you feel good about yourself! That's what it is all about. Having someone who makes you laugh and who, no matter how many times you've seen each other, still makes your heart skip a beat when he walks in to the room. He has to respect you! He has to put your heart before his own. He has to make you his queen so that even when the whole world tells you you're worthless he is right there to pick up the pieces and make you whole again. He has to do those things for you, and you have to do those things for him. Things are still going to be hard—the only difference is that every ounce of work that you put into it makes everything worth it because he is the guy you can't live without.

If you are currently with someone who doesn't make you feel good about yourself, please get the biggest pair of emotional scissors you can and cut him out of your life. I have lived this. I am not just telling you what someone else told me. I am telling you this because if I can save one person from the emotional ruin I have found myself in over and over again than everything I went through was worth it. Don't be like me. Don't keep selling yourself short or waiting on his potential or settling for good. Take control of your life because only you can. It really kills me to see great women sticking with awful men. You need to see the beauty that is you. If you're a skinny, beautiful Barbie® doll and he treats you like nothing but a pretty object, get out of there. You have so much to offer intellectually, and you may not even know it because you've been living in his shadow for so long.

If you're overweight and he is constantly telling you that not only are you too big but that you couldn't do better than him if you wanted to, it's time to say goodbye. Then, if you want to—because this is your body and your choice—lose weight and get to a size that makes you feel beautiful. It's all about learning to love yourself and feeling confident in who you are. Once you're happy, go and find someone else who loves you for who you are. You were not created to be anyone else's whipping post, stomping ground, or pet. In your veins pumps the power of a woman. Women are so important to God that He knew the world could not continue to turn on its axis unless He knelt down and formed us. You're important, and it's time you realize it.

As I close this book, I urge you to let God guide you as you prepare yourself for your soul mate. May you find nothing but love, peace, and happiness. I hope to meet you in heaven one day and hear all about how everything worked out. This is my prayer for you:

Dear Lord, I ask that You bless this child of Yours and keep her heart in the palm of Your hand. I pray that she lives a life that brings glory to Your name so that when You return You will grab her hand and whisper, "Well done, my good and faithful servant!" Bless her in her search for her soul mate, Father, because I know nothing escapes Your attention. Love her through all the hardships she will encounter, Lord, and mark her as Yours forever. Amen.

Now, what are you waiting for? Get out there and listen for thunder!

Sexual Purity Contract

This contract is designed to help me stay sexually pure until my wedding day.

**Because of my love and faith in Jesus Christ,
I am going to wait until I am married to share my body
and soul with the man God created with me in mind.**

My body is a temple, and I want to preserve this most precious
gift for my wedding night, when the man who has decided to stand
before my family and God to take me as his wife is ready
to reap all the beauty of our love through the physical act of sex.

I am waiting for him because I am beautiful and precious
and because I deserve to feel the intimacy of real love.

With love,

Signature: _____

Print Name: _____